THE PASTORAL EPISTLES

Founding Principles · Faithful Practice · Finishing Well

A Pastoral Commentary on
1 & 2 Timothy and Titus

by Joseph Edwards-Hoff

Copyright

ISBN 978-1-971665-00-9

Published by

Joseph Edwards-Hoff

Grandview, Washington

Printed in the United States of America

Dedication

To my wife and children,

You all have borne the weight of ministry with patience. You continually remind me that the truth of Scripture must be lived before it is ever taught. You are my greatest joy and my greatest responsibility.

To my assisting pastor, who has helped me tirelessly with the commitment of bringing the Word of God to the men and women of our church.

To the saints of Revival Church, for whom the Pastoral Epistles are not theory, but life. Thank you for your kind words, your faithful service, and most of all, your growing faith. "I have no greater joy than to hear that my children walk in truth."

Finally, to faithful pastors who labor unseen, yet must finish well. It is a hard road that we tread, but it is a worthy one.

About the Author

Joseph Edwards-Hoff is the pastor of Revival Church in Grandview, Washington, where he serves with a deep commitment to the local church, expository preaching, and the authority of God's Word. His ministry has been shaped not only by years of teaching and shepherding, but by the daily realities of leading a church, raising a family, and laboring to finish well.

Joseph's teaching emphasizes careful attention to the biblical text, historical context, and theological clarity, with a consistent focus on faithful application. He believes the truths of Scripture are meant to shape real lives in real churches, and that doctrine divorced from obedience ultimately fails The Church it claims to serve.

He is married to his wife, Nicole, and together they are raising their seven children. Much of Joseph's pastoral theology has been formed in the ordinary, often unseen work of family life and local church ministry, where faithfulness is tested not in theory, but in practice.

How to Use This Commentary

This commentary is written for all students of Scripture—whether pastors, teachers, or devout Christians—who desire to understand the Word of God more clearly and live it more faithfully. While it is well suited for teaching and preaching, it is not written exclusively for pastor teachers, nor does it assume formal theological training.

The New King James Version (NKJV) is used by default unless otherwise noted. Greek words are included where they help clarify meaning, though no prior knowledge of Greek is assumed. These word studies are intended to serve the reader and deepen understanding, not to distract from the flow of the text.

The approach throughout is exegetical and pastoral. Historical background, grammar, and theology are handled in service of understanding the passage as it was originally given, and then applying it faithfully within the life of The Church. Illustrations and pastoral observations are included to demonstrate how sound doctrine must shape real obedience.

This commentary is best read slowly and thoughtfully. Readers may work through it consecutively or consult individual sections as needed, allowing the text of Scripture to set the pace and direction of study.

Table of Contents

Introduction

The Pastoral Epistles—1 Timothy, 2 Timothy, and Titus—
were written near the end of the apostle Paul's life and
were letters written by a seasoned pastor to younger men
who were carrying out real responsibilities in real churches.
Paul is not dealing with doctrinal theory here. He is
concerned with truth that must be guarded, lives that must
be ordered, and faith that must endure to the end.

The material you are reading was first delivered as sermons
to the local church I pastor in. It was shaped in the ordinary
rhythm of church life—teaching the Word week after week,
answering questions as they arose, and applying Scripture
to people who were trying to live faithfully in a difficult
world.

Because of that, the structure of this commentary follows
the flow of those sermons rather than strict chapter
divisions. The text is handled in the units that were taught,
which allows certain themes to be developed slowly and
carefully. Some passages receive extended attention, while
others are treated more briefly. At times, important truths
are revisited. This is intentional. Pastoral instruction is not
rushed, and it often requires repetition.

Nothing in this work is meant to replace careful study of
the biblical text. Rather, it is meant to model how Scripture
is to be handled in the life of The Church—explained
clearly, applied honestly, and pressed into everyday
obedience. The goal is not simply to know what Paul wrote,
but to live in light of it. These letters call the Church to
hold fast to sound doctrine, to live in a way that reflects the
Gospel, and to finish well. That call has not changed. My
prayer is that this commentary would help readers
understand the Pastoral Epistles more clearly and walk in
their teachings more faithfully.

The Charge to Timothy
1 Timothy 1:1-2:7

Introduction: What Happened to Paul After Acts 28?

The book of First Timothy opens a window into a period of Paul's life not covered in the Book of Acts. First Timothy, Titus, and Second Timothy—written in that order—are the last three letters Paul penned, and he wrote them after the events of Acts conclude. Piecing together a timeline requires careful detective work, gathering clues scattered throughout these final epistles.

At the end of Acts 28, Paul is in Rome under house arrest for two years. The real question is: what happened next?

Based on references throughout his letters, one proposed reconstruction of Paul's movements looks something like this: After his release from his first Roman imprisonment around AD 62–63, he visited Crete, where he left Titus. He visited Colossae—we know this because in Philemon he writes, "Prepare a guest room for me" (Philemon 22). He told the Philippians he hoped to see them soon (Philippians 1:25; 2:24). At some point he swung through Ephesus multiple times, and on one of those trips he left Timothy there. Whether he wrote First Timothy and Titus before or after his time in Spain is difficult to determine.

Church tradition holds that Paul spent one or two years in Spain. Romans 15:24 records his explicit desire to go there, and early church fathers such as Clement of Rome confirm he made it. On his return trip east, he made additional stops. In Second Timothy he mentions leaving items in

Miletus, Troas, and Corinth, telling people to retrieve things he left along the way (2 Timothy 4:13, 20).

What we know for certain is that Second Timothy was written just before Paul's death in AD 67–68. Everything else falls somewhere in between his release and that final imprisonment.

It is also worth noting that John apparently had not yet arrived in Ephesus during this period. Around AD 66, when Rome began its assault on Jerusalem, Christians remembered Jesus's warning in Luke 21 to flee when they saw these things coming to pass. Tradition holds that not a single Christian was killed when over a million Jews were slaughtered in Jerusalem in AD 70—because they remembered the Lord's words and escaped. John, along with Mary the mother of Jesus, went to Ephesus. They likely did not arrive until AD 66 or 67. If they had been there earlier, one would expect Paul to mention them in First or Second Timothy, letters addressed to Ephesus. But there is no mention. By the time John and Mary arrived, Paul was probably already imprisoned again and unaware of their presence.

That provides some background to the writing of these epistles—Paul writing to Timothy and Titus, two of his most trusted young followers.

The Theme of the Pastoral Epistles

If there is a theme verse for First Timothy—and really for all three Pastoral Epistles—it is found in chapter 3:

> *"But if I am delayed, I write so that you may know how you ought to conduct yourself in the house of God, which is The Church of*

> *the living God, the pillar and ground of the*
> *truth." (1 Timothy 3:15)*

Paul is essentially providing instructions for how to do church. Timothy and Titus were pastors, which is why these letters are called the Pastoral Epistles. They were written to them personally, but they were also intended for the whole church to hear.

Timothy held a unique place in Paul's ministry. In Philippians, Paul writes:

> *"But I trust in the Lord Jesus to send*
> *Timothy to you shortly, that I also may be*
> *encouraged when I know your state. For I*
> *have no one like-minded, who will sincerely*
> *care for your state." (Philippians 2:19–20)*

There was no one as like-minded with Paul as Timothy. He was Paul's number one.

The Greeting: Grace, Mercy, and Peace

> *"Paul, an apostle of Jesus Christ, by the*
> *commandment of God our Savior and the*
> *Lord Jesus Christ, our hope, to Timothy, a*
> *true son in the faith: Grace, mercy, and*
> *peace from God our Father and Jesus Christ*
> *our Lord." (1 Timothy 1:1–2)*

This is strong wording. Writing to Timothy—his closest ministry partner—Paul uses emphatic language about his apostolic authority: "by the commandment of God." Timothy probably did not need to hear this, but the people who would be receiving Timothy's instruction certainly did. Timothy was going to deliver some tough messages, and Paul wanted everyone to know these words carried

3

apostolic weight. This was coming straight down the line from Jesus Christ.

Paul calls God "our Savior," which is actually uncommon in the New Testament. Typically Scripture refers to "Jesus our Savior," yet here he calls Jesus Christ "our hope." Jesus is our blessed hope. As Christians, He must be our hope— not money, not spouses, not the president, not any political leader. America is not the last great hope of the world. Jesus is our hope. If America is the last great hope of the world, we are in trouble. But if Jesus is our hope, and America continues to embrace Him more and more, that would be wonderful. And if The Church gets raptured and America is simply emptied of believers—that would be a great explanation for why America does not appear prominently in end times prophecy.

Paul addresses Timothy as "a true son in the faith"—a genuine son, not merely a title of affection but an accurate description of their relationship.

Then comes the greeting: "Grace, mercy, and peace from God our Father and Jesus Christ our Lord." In most of Paul's letters, the greeting is "grace and peace"—grace before peace, because you cannot have the peace of God until you have received the grace of God. But only in the Pastoral Epistles—only to the pastors—does Paul add "mercy." Grace, mercy, and peace. Perhaps it is because he is writing to a brother in ministry, someone who knows the unique pains of pastoral work. Of all people, pastors need mercy.

Grace is getting what you do not deserve. Mercy is not getting what you do deserve. Picture being caught red-handed, standing before a judge with mountains of evidence proving guilt for a horrific crime. The judge looks at the defendant and says, "I am throwing it out." That is mercy—the guilty party did not deserve to have the case dismissed. But then, to make things even more extraordinary, the judge says, "Come with me." He changes the prisoner out of prison clothes, buys a new suit, drives to a beautiful house. He hands over the keys to the car, the keys to the house, and then adoption papers. "I want you to be my son." That is grace. Not only forgiven but receiving what was never earned. That is mercy and grace together.

The Charge: Stop the False Teaching

> *"As I urged you when I went into*
> *Macedonia, remain in Ephesus that you may*
> *charge some that they teach no other*
> *doctrine, nor give heed to fables and endless*
> *genealogies, which cause disputes rather*
> *than godly edification which is in faith."*
> *(1 Timothy 1:3–4)*

This verse helps piece together Paul's travels. He went to Ephesus, left Timothy there, and headed to Macedonia— where Philippi, Berea, and Thessalonica were located. But more importantly, it reveals a threat of false teaching infiltrating the Ephesian church.

Paul had warned about this in his letter to the Ephesians. By the time John writes Revelation some thirty years later, Jesus commends the Ephesian church for being doctrinally solid—for knowing how to reject what is false and approve what is good (Revelation 2:2). Obviously, Paul's letters, Timothy's ministry, and later John's leadership accomplished their purpose. They did a good job guarding against "other doctrine."

Just like in many of Paul's other epistles, the primary threat here seems to be the Judaizers. The Judaizers were Jewish Christians who insisted that Gentile believers must follow the Mosaic Law—particularly circumcision and dietary laws—in order to truly be devout Christians. They were a persistent problem in the early church, and much of Paul's letter to the Galatians was written to counter their teaching. Their error was adding works to grace, making the ideal Christian life contingent on law-keeping rather than faith alone in Christ.

It is not as explicit here as in Galatians, which addresses the issue head-on, but as the chapter progresses, the evidence becomes clear. Paul warns later in this letter:

> *"Now the Spirit expressly says that in latter times some will depart from the faith, giving heed to deceiving spirits and doctrines of demons." (1 Timothy 4:1)*

Look at The Church today. Are there not absolutely crazy things being taught in places that call themselves churches, by people who call themselves Christians? It is maddening. It is insane. But Paul said it. Peter said it. The Bible says it again and again: do not be surprised. In the latter days, they will depart from the faith. In the latter days, they will grow cold. In the latter days, there will be doctrines of demons and deceiving spirits. We should not be surprised that the Bible is proving true.

Paul specifies "fables and endless genealogies" as part of the problem. The word for fables is *mythos (μῦθος)*—the Greek word from which we get "myth." In Titus, Paul mentions "Jewish fables and commandments of men who turn from the truth" (Titus 1:14). These seem to be similar issues: Jewish myths and man-made rules being imposed on believers.

The "endless genealogies" likely involve people tracing Jewish ancestry—perhaps claiming that having Jewish blood makes one superior or speculating about descent from various tribes. Paul says this kind of thing "causes disputes rather than godly edification which is in faith." Nitpicking little things, getting caught up on the Law—it sounds silly when you hear about the rabbis debating how many angels can fit on the head of a needle. That was an actual rabbinical discussion, which is why the phrase exists today. But there are churches doing the same thing now, trying to pin everything down into law rather than living by grace.

Here is the thing: when you have the Holy Spirit living inside you, you do not need endless rules. The Spirit convicts and guides. There is no need to create a law saying, "do not do drugs," because if someone has the Holy Spirit inside, He is eventually going to point them in the right direction.

The Purpose of the Charge: Love

"Now the purpose of the commandment is love from a pure heart, from a good conscience, and from sincere faith."
(1 Timothy 1:5)

An important note: the word "commandment" here is *parangelia (παραγγελία)* in Greek. This word is never used in the New Testament for the Mosaic commandments. It is better translated "charge" or "instruction" the same concept from verse 3, where Paul charged Timothy to stop false teaching and ensure good teaching continues.

Some have tried to argue that this verse means following the Mosaic Law stirs up love. That is not what Paul is saying. The charge to stop false doctrine and maintain sound doctrine—that charge has a purpose, and the purpose is love from a pure heart, a good conscience, and sincere faith.

One of my favorite pastors often says, "Doctrine is important because right beliefs produce right behavior." That captures the idea here. Paul emphasizes that correct doctrine and the stopping of false doctrine serve a greater end. The goal is not to become the most theologically accurate church in town just to pat ourselves on the back for knowing things. Doctrine simply means "what we believe." Teaching right beliefs and stopping false beliefs stirs up love.

This is not about getting people to memorize theology for the sake of memorization. The deeper we go into the Word, the deeper the meaning becomes. Understanding the culture, the geography, the historical context—it all helps the Bible come alive with richer significance. But ultimately, doctrine stirs up love. It stirs up a pure heart and a good conscience.

As Paul writes elsewhere, Christ is "washing His bride with the water of the word, that He might present her to Himself a glorious church, not having spot or wrinkle or any such thing" (Ephesians 5:26–27). The washing of the water of the Word is the most direct biblical path to sanctification. Psalm 119:9 asks, "How can a young man cleanse his way?" The answer: "By taking heed according to Your word."

Swerving into Vain Jangling

"From which some, having strayed, have turned aside to idle talk." (1 Timothy 1:6)

The King James Version renders this beautifully: "From which some having swerved have turned aside unto vain jangling." Vain jangling. That phrase deserves a comeback.

Imagine the image it conjures; driving along, swerving to dodge something, and suddenly hitting things left and right—running over cones, ding, ding, ding. These people were on course with solid biblical teaching, the doctrine that has been around for two thousand years. The majority of The Church still holds to the apostles' teaching. Then fringe groups and cultists come along with something new, revolutionary, completely different from what has been taught for two millennia. That is swerving, and it ends in vain jangling—a lot of noise about nothing.

If it is true, it is not new. If it is new, it is not true. There is wisdom in that saying. Solomon said there is nothing new under the sun (Ecclesiastes 1:9). The main thing has stayed the main thing for two thousand years in the majority of The Church.

Teachers of the Law

> *"Desiring to be teachers of the law,*
> *understanding neither what they say nor the*
> *things which they affirm." (1 Timothy 1:7)*

Here is where we know for certain we are dealing with Judaizers. The phrase "teachers of the law" is a specific term: *nomodidaskalos (νομοδιδάσκαλος)* in Greek—literally "law teacher," combining *nomos* (law) and *didaskalos* (teacher). In the New Testament, this term is always used specifically of teachers of the Mosaic Law.

In Luke 5:17, when the paralytic was lowered through the roof, the Pharisees had law teachers with them. Acts 5:34 calls Gamaliel a law teacher—he was one of the most respected rabbis of his age. Luke sometimes uses the term "lawyers" as a synonym for these same people.

9

This word is very specific. These were not general teachers; they were people who wanted to become teachers of the Mosaic Law, putting Gentiles under it. But look what Paul says about them: they understand "neither what they say nor the things which they affirm." They want to impose the Law, but they have no idea what they are talking about.

The Law Is Good—If Used Lawfully

> *"But we know that the law is good if one uses it lawfully, knowing this: that the law is not made for a righteous person, but for the lawless and insubordinate, for the ungodly and for sinners, for the unholy and profane, for murderers of fathers and murderers of mothers, for manslayers, for fornicators, for sodomites, for kidnappers, for liars, for perjurers, and if there is any other thing that is contrary to sound doctrine, according to the glorious gospel of the blessed God which was committed to my trust." (1 Timothy 1:8–11)*

This is a straightforward statement: the Law of Moses is still good. It has never become bad—as long as you understand its proper place.

Much of the Old Testament contains commands to the Israelites that do not apply to believers today. No one will ever march around Jericho banging pots and pans to make walls fall down, because that Jericho no longer exists. But the story of Joshua is still edifying. Tremendous lessons come from it.

Even the ceremonial laws have value when understood properly. Christians are permitted to wear mixed fabrics—wool and cotton in the same outfit. The Jews were not

(Leviticus 19:19). Is that unimportant? No, because it is a beautiful picture. God made them do certain things to show they were not to be a mixed people, not to be unequally yoked. The principle carries over even if the specific command does not apply.

The Law of Moses is good if we understand its place and how to use it. How can the Law be used lawfully? Paul explains: "The law is not made for a righteous person, but for the lawless and insubordinate." The Law is not here for righteous people to follow as a means of achieving righteousness. It is for showing the unrighteous their sin.

Ray Comfort and his Way of the Master ministry demonstrate this beautifully in evangelism. They take people through the Law: Have you ever told a lie? Have you ever taken the Lord's name in vain? Have you ever stolen anything? Walking through the commandments, people realize they are guilty. "You are a lying, thieving blasphemer, an adulterer at heart—and you think you are going to heaven?" The Law shows people they would be guilty before a righteous Judge. That is using the Law lawfully.

There is something fascinating about Paul's list here. It actually echoes the Ten Commandments. Set side by side, the alignment becomes clear:

"Lawless and insubordinate" — "No other gods."
"Ungodly and sinners" — "No graven images."
"Unholy and profane" — "Blasphemy" and "The Sabbath."
"Murderers of fathers and mothers" — "Honor father and mother."
"Manslayers" — "Do not murder."
"Fornicators and sodomites" — "Do not commit adultery."
"Kidnappers" — "Do not steal."

11

"Liars and perjurers" — "Do not bear false witness."
"Any other thing" — "Do not covet."

The second half of the Ten Commandments lines up remarkably well. Paul is showing that the Law reveals people's transgressions and their need for God's mercy and grace.

Paul's Testimony of Grace

> *"And I thank Christ Jesus our Lord who has enabled me, because He counted me faithful, putting me into the ministry, although I was formerly a blasphemer, a persecutor, and an insolent man; but I obtained mercy because I did it ignorantly in unbelief."*
> *(1 Timothy 1:12–13)*

Paul recognized he was a minister by grace alone. He did not work his way up to becoming an apostle. It was the mercy of God.

This is a good reminder for anyone in ministry: seminaries and certificates do not make someone a pastor. Even the laying on of hands by elders does not make someone a pastor—their job is to acknowledge God's calling, because God does the calling. This is true for all ministry. God calls and places people where He designed them to serve. Every believer is part of the body of Christ, fearfully and wonderfully made with a purpose.

As Paul addresses these law teachers, he makes a powerful point. Paul had a radical conversion. Before Christ, he was a radical Jew who followed the Law flawlessly—he tells the Philippians he was blameless according to the Law (Philippians 3:6). If anyone could have been justified by law-keeping, it was Paul. Yet he tells these Judaizers: when

I was zealous for the Law, I was a blasphemer, a persecutor, an insolent man. Then I obtained mercy. Now I am simply thankful that He counted me faithful and put me into ministry.

Rules never stir up love. Churches built on rules—even ones preaching a saving gospel—can become legalistic, imposing standards and commandments that are not biblical. That does not produce love. But when God calls someone out of the mire—out of drugs, out of sexual sin, out of drunkenness, out of selfishness, out of being grumpy and mean—when He saves, washes, and makes new, it stirs up love. It stirs up zeal and a desire for good works. Good works do not make someone a good Christian. A good God who loved us stirs up good works within us.

Paul writes to the Corinthians with a similar list of sins— fornicators, idolaters, adulterers, homosexuals, thieves, covetous, drunkards, revilers, extortioners—and then declares:

> *"And such were some of you. But you were washed, but you were sanctified, but you were justified in the name of the Lord Jesus and by the Spirit of our God." (1 Corinthians 6:11)*

When someone becomes a Christian, they are no longer those things. They *formerly* were those things. You cannot be a drunkard Christian. You may be a Christian who struggles with alcoholism, but you are not defined as a drunkard. You are not a murderer Christian or a fornicating Christian. You are washed, made new. Even if you struggle or stumble in those areas, they no longer define you. Paul was formerly a blasphemer and persecutor, but that no longer defined who he was. He was now a Christian, in Christ.

13

> *"And the grace of our Lord was exceedingly abundant, with faith and love which are in Christ Jesus." (1 Timothy 1:14)*

A Faithful Saying

> *"This is a faithful saying and worthy of all acceptance, that Christ Jesus came into the world to save sinners, of whom I am chief."*
> *(1 Timothy 1:15)*

The phrase "this is a faithful saying and worthy of all acceptance" appears several times in the Pastoral Epistles. It became almost a theological formula in the early church—a way of saying, "What I am about to tell you is critically important and should be memorized by everyone." If you forget everything else, do not forget this: Christ Jesus came into the world to save sinners.

Paul calls himself "chief" of sinners. In the Greek, it is actually "a chief"—not claiming to be the absolute worst sinner who ever lived, but saying that among all the worst sinners, he was right there with them. And Christ came and saved him.

> *"However, for this reason I obtained mercy, that in me first Jesus Christ might show all longsuffering, as a pattern to those who are going to believe on Him for everlasting life."*
> *(1 Timothy 1:16)*

Sometimes we wonder why God allows us to experience certain things. We go through pain, suffering, trials, hardships—and we wonder why. Paul writes elsewhere that the God of all comfort comforts us in our trials so that we may comfort others with the comfort we have received (2 Corinthians 1:3–4). Sometimes God is teaching us how to reach people. There are hurt and lost people who are not saved. Believers have been saved, but those lost people are going through similar pain. Having walked through that suffering, a believer can reach them in ways no one else could.

It is sobering to consider: if some of the pain I have experienced was just to win one soul, was it worth it? If that soul is your daughter, your son, your spouse—absolutely it is worth it. You may have lost everything, but that one person gained everything because God had a plan to use you and the things you went through.

Consider what Paul had done. He was a zealous persecutor of The Church. Acts tells us he was causing Christians to blaspheme at the point of the sword (Acts 26:11). He was present when Stephen was martyred, holding the coats of those who stoned him (Acts 7:58). He was involved in the deaths of Christians.

Many of my high school friends served in Iraq—Mosul, Fallujah, all the major combat zones. They came back with startling stories. Similar to accounts from more recent persecutions—ISIS, Hamas, terrorist organizations. Husbands forced to watch their wives violated and killed before being martyred themselves. Children tortured to make families renounce Christ.

While teaching through Acts with the youth group, I looked up the news from that week. The story was about a twelve-year-old boy. His father had to watch as every finger was slowly broken, trying to get the boy and the father to renounce Jesus Christ. They would not do it. The boy was martyred. The father was martyred. They never turned away from their faith.

15

The wicked, evil people who did that—that is who Paul was. That is what he was doing. He was hunting down Christians at the point of the sword, trying to get them to renounce their faith. And God saved him. Paul obtained mercy, and now he stands as a model showing everyone that no one is beyond saving. No one is beyond God's mercy. Whatever you have done—and some reading this have done terrible things—it is unlikely any have murdered people trying to force them to renounce their faith. Paul did. And God saved him as an example for all who would believe after him.

A Doxology

> *"Now to the King eternal, immortal,*
> *invisible, to God who alone is wise, be*
> *honor and glory forever and ever. Amen."*
> *(1 Timothy 1:17)*

After reflecting on what God did for him, Paul breaks into a doxology. The Greek word for glory is *doxa*, so a doxology is simply something that gives glory to God. Those who grew up in churches with liturgy may remember singing the Doxology—"Praise God from whom all blessings flow"— or the Gloria Patri—"Glory be to the Father." These are doxologies. Scripture contains many of them—at the end of Jude, in Romans, here in First Timothy. They are bursts of praise that cannot be contained.

Paul is so overwhelmed with gratitude that he erupts in worship: to the King eternal, immortal, invisible, to God who alone is wise, be honor and glory forever.

The Charge to Timothy

"This charge I commit to you, son Timothy,
according to the prophecies previously
made concerning you, that by them you may
wage the good warfare, having faith and a
good conscience, which some having
rejected, concerning the faith have suffered
shipwreck." (1 Timothy 1:18–19)

The charge is to stop false teaching and ensure good teaching continues. Paul reminds Timothy of prophecies spoken over him. Later in this letter, Paul writes: "Do not neglect the gift that is in you, which was given to you by prophecy with the laying on of the hands of the eldership" (1 Timothy 4:14). When Timothy was called to ministry, the elders gathered around him, laid hands on him, prayed, and apparently prophesied over him—declaring what God would do through him.

Scholars generally agree that Timothy was probably a timid person. The exhortations throughout First and Second Timothy suggest he needed continual encouragement. He was not a bold go-getter like Paul. Paul is reminding him: Do not forget the prophecy, Timothy. That prophecy is going to come true. Hold fast. Believe that you can put your foot down and stop these false teachers. By those prophecies, wage the good warfare.

If you do not have specific prophecies spoken over you, remember that we all have the Word of God. Scripture makes prophetic statements about all believers. Worried about sanctification? "Be confident of this very thing, that He who has begun a good work in you will complete it until the day of Jesus Christ" (Philippians 1:6). The Word of God encourages us to wage good warfare.

17

Some, Paul says, rejected faith and a good conscience, and their faith shipwrecked. They were with The Church for a season but veered off into vain jangling. As John writes in his first epistle, "They went out from us, but they were not of us; for if they had been of us, they would have continued with us; but they went out that they might be made manifest, that none of them were of us" (1 John 2:19).

Naming Names

> *"Of whom are Hymenaeus and Alexander,*
> *whom I delivered to Satan that they may*
> *learn not to blaspheme." (1 Timothy 1:20)*

Paul names names. There are two sides to this. One guy from our church is always telling me, "Name names, Pastor. Just say who it is." But typically, naming names publicly requires careful consideration.

First, remember this was a letter to a church where everyone knew the situation. In that context, it was appropriate to warn people: stay away from these individuals; they will lead you astray. Imagine if someone in a local church was creating division and spreading false teaching. It would be wise and healthy to identify them so the congregation knows to be cautious.

Second, we should be very tactful about naming names publicly. Slander is a sin whether intended or not. Something shared thinking it was true, if it turns out to be false, becomes slander—and that is on the one who shared it. If someone is going to name names and share things publicly, they need to be absolutely certain what they are sharing is true.

We know more about Hymenaeus from Second Timothy:

"Shun profane and idle babblings, for they
will increase to more ungodliness. And their
message will spread like cancer. Hymenaeus
and Philetus are of this sort, who have
strayed concerning the truth, saying that the
resurrection is already past; and they
overthrow the faith of some."
(2 Timothy 2:16–18)

Hymenaeus was teaching that the resurrection had already
happened. This teaching still exists today under the
theological term "full preterism"—the belief that all
biblical prophecy, including the resurrection and second
coming, has already been fulfilled. Some believe the entire
book of Revelation symbolically describes events leading
to the destruction of Jerusalem in AD 70, and that there is
no future heaven, no new heavens and earth, no bodily
resurrection to come.

The early church condemned this as heresy. The Second
Council of Constantinople in AD 553 addressed similar
issues regarding the resurrection. There are many respected
teachers who hold to "partial preterism"—believing most
prophecy has been fulfilled but that Christ will still return.
That is a debatable position, though I disagree with it
regarding prophecy. But full preterism is different. It denies
heaven, the resurrection, and the future return of Christ. It
approaches the level of seriousness of denying the deity of
Christ.

Hymenaeus was teaching this—that the resurrection had
already passed. Since Revelation was not yet written,
perhaps he would have figured it out eventually.
Regardless, his teaching was dangerous enough that Paul
took drastic action.

19

Delivered to Satan

What does it mean to "deliver someone to Satan"? The only other occurrence of this phrase is in First Corinthians:

> *"Deliver such a one to Satan for the destruction of the flesh, that his spirit may be saved in the day of the Lord Jesus." (1 Corinthians 5:5)*

Delivering someone to Satan does not mean killing them. It does not mean sending them to hell. It means removing them from The Church. Who is the god of this world? Satan holds that title (2 Corinthians 4:4). Within The Church—within this body, this family—there is protection and blessing. Being among believers provides spiritual covering.

Years ago, in the town I was living in, there was a homeless man who seemed to be possessed by demons. He would speak in different languages, different tones—a whole spectrum of disturbing behavior. But something interesting happened whenever Christians got near him: it would all stop instantly. Other people could talk to him and he would still be erratic. But when believers came around, the presence of the Holy Spirit inside them seemed to have power. This is not a universal formula, but it illustrates the point: there is protection and power in the community of believers.

When someone becomes spiritually cancerous—spreading false teaching and refusing to repent—they are removed from that protection. Paul uses the same imagery in First Corinthians 5: "A little leaven leavens the whole lump" (1 Corinthians 5:6). Like cancer, false teaching spreads. It must be removed before it infects everything.

This was not punishment for punishment's sake. It had a redemptive purpose: "that his spirit may be saved." The goal was to put the unrepentant persons out into the world where Satan could buffet them, hoping they would come to their senses and return to The Church with a repentant heart.

This discipline is reserved for the unrepentant—those who refuse to listen to correction. The man in First Corinthians 5 was sleeping with his stepmother. The church confronted him. He refused to change. Eventually they removed him. But later, in Second Corinthians, we learn that he repented and was restored. Paul actually had to warn The Church not to be too harsh—to welcome him back, lest Satan use their hard hearts to create unnecessary division (2 Corinthians 2:5–11).

A Note on Matthew 18

In Matthew 18, when Jesus says, "Where two or three are gathered in My name, I am there in the midst of them" (Matthew 18:20), He is not giving us a warm devotional thought about small group meetings.

That verse comes at the end of Jesus's teaching on church discipline. The context begins in verse 15: "If your brother sins against you, go and tell him his fault between you and him alone." If he will not hear, take one or two more. If he still refuses to listen, tell it to The Church. If he refuses to hear even The Church, "let him be to you like a heathen and a tax collector" (Matthew 18:17).

Then Jesus says, "Assuredly, I say to you, whatever you bind on earth will be bound in heaven, and whatever you loose on earth will be loosed in heaven. Again I say to you that if two of you agree on earth concerning anything that they ask, it will be done for them by My Father in heaven.

21

For where two or three are gathered together in My name, I am there in the midst of them" (Matthew 18:18–20).

Jesus is assuring church leaders that when they must make difficult decisions together—decisions about discipline, about removing unrepentant people—He is with them and backing them up. It is not a promise about worship attendance minimums. It is a promise about authority in church discipline.

Prayer for All Men

Having addressed false teaching and church discipline, Paul turns to practical instruction for The Church.

> *"Therefore I exhort first of all that*
> *supplications, prayers, intercessions, and*
> *giving of thanks be made for all men, for*
> *kings and all who are in authority, that we*
> *may lead a quiet and peaceable life in all*
> *godliness and reverence." (1 Timothy 2:1–2)*

Paul uses four different words for prayer here—supplications, prayers, intercessions, thanksgiving—not to distinguish four rigid categories, but to emphasize comprehensiveness. All types of prayer should be made for all men.

And in the Greek, "all" means all. We should pray for everyone—friends and enemies, people we like and people we do not like, leaders we support and leaders we oppose. We should still be praying for presidents after they leave office. We should be praying for governors, mayors, school boards, city councils, principals—everyone with influence in our communities.

Sometimes Christians talk about people in authority in ways that raise the question of whether they pray for them at all. It is much easier to obey and respect leaders when praying for them. And it is hard to speak with contempt about people being lifted up in prayer.

Even an incompetent leader—and history has provided more than one—looks different when prayer focuses on their lostness, their deception, their eternal destiny. Praying for their salvation changes the heart toward them.

The goal of prayer is not merely self-interested: "Lord, handle this person so I can have a comfortable life." We are to pray genuinely for them. Imagine if they got saved and experienced radical transformation. If we pray sincerely for the salvation and blessing of those in authority, and God works in their hearts, we will experience the byproduct: a quiet and peaceable life.

The Greek words for "quiet" and "peaceable" are interesting. "Quiet" refers to freedom from disturbances without; "peaceable" refers to freedom from disturbances within. Together they encompass complete peace—outward and inward.

God Desires All to Be Saved

"For this is good and acceptable in the sight of God our Savior, who desires all men to be saved and to come to the knowledge of the truth." (1 Timothy 2:3–4)

Why pray for all men? Because God our Savior desires all men to be saved and come to the knowledge of the truth. Praying for all people is doing His will.

23

Note carefully: God *desires* all men to be saved. He is not failing to accomplish something He is attempting to do. "To be saved" is passive in the Greek. The idea is that He desires these men would *come* to salvation—not be forced, not have it happen by chance, but come willingly.

One God, One Mediator

> *"For there is one God and one Mediator*
> *between God and men, the Man Christ*
> *Jesus, who gave Himself a ransom for all, to*
> *be testified in due time." (1 Timothy 2:5–6)*

We pray for all men because there is only one God for them all to turn to, and they need to know that one God. We pray for all men because there is only one Mediator, and most people have the wrong one. If they are pursuing other gods, they have the wrong God. If they think there is some other way to the Father, they have the wrong way. Jesus said, "I am the way, the truth, and the life. No one comes to the Father except through Me" (John 14:6).

Jesus gave Himself a ransom for all. Matthew records that the Son of Man came "to give His life a ransom for many" (Matthew 20:28). Here Paul says it even more inclusively: a ransom for all. First John is explicit:

> *"He Himself is the propitiation for our sins,*
> *and not for ours only but also for the whole*
> *world." (1 John 2:2)*

Jesus paid it all. He made the payment for all mankind. But we know that not all will be saved, because, as John's Gospel says, the darkness loved the darkness and would not come to the light lest its deeds be exposed (John 3:19–20). The payment is made and available to all; not all will receive it.

I once told the youth group: Imagine I bought each of you an iPhone. They are here, wrapped with bows, your names on them. They are purchased and paid for. It is my desire that you take them. Now if you do not show up to receive yours, whose fault is that? If you show up but refuse to pick it up, whose fault is that? The gift is bought. Your name is on it. But you must come and receive it.

That is the gospel. Christ purchased salvation for all. But this by no means implies universalism—that everyone will be saved. If everyone were automatically saved, there would be no need for God to *desire* that all men be saved.

The Man Christ Jesus

The text emphasizes "the Man Christ Jesus." In the Greek, it could be rendered "a man, Christ Jesus." Paul is painting a picture his readers would have understood. Job lamented:

> *"For He is not a man, as I am, that I may answer Him, and that we should go to court together. Nor is there any mediator between us, who may lay his hand on us both." (Job 9:32–33)*

If you understand the glory of God, you understand the problem. God is so holy, so righteous, so powerful—how could anyone ever approach Him? Everyone who sees God in Scripture falls flat on their face. Isaiah cries, "Woe is me, for I am undone!" (Isaiah 6:5).

But if there were a man—someone I could relate to, someone who knew my experiences and was touched with my weaknesses—that is someone I could approach boldly, someone who could go on my behalf to that holy God and lay his hand on us both.

This is not merely emphasizing that Jesus was a man, though that is true. It is a reminder that He was *fully* man—fully God and fully man. As Hebrews says, "We do not have a High Priest who cannot sympathize with our weaknesses, but was in all points tempted as we are, yet without sin" (Hebrews 4:15). He knows what we have gone through. And He is the only Mediator.

You cannot pray to angels. You cannot pray to dead saints—not Paul, not Peter, not Mary, not anyone. There is one Mediator between God and men: Jesus Christ. He is the one who lays His hand on both parties, connecting us to the Father.

Paul's Calling

> *"For which I was appointed a preacher and an apostle—I am speaking the truth in Christ and not lying—a teacher of the Gentiles in faith and truth." (1 Timothy 2:7)*

Paul concludes this section by affirming his calling. He was appointed to teach people about Jesus and this glorious gospel—the gospel of mercy, grace, truth, love, and freedom.

Any gospel that adds rules not found in Scripture is not a freeing gospel; it is an enslaving gospel. Any gospel that does not set us free from sin—where people keep living in sin while claiming belief—is not the true gospel either. The gospel frees us from sin so we can live unashamed before Him.

That is the message Paul was called to proclaim, and that is the message Timothy was charged to protect.

Church Leadership
1 Timothy 2:8-3:15

Timothy is receiving instructions from Paul the Apostle. He is overseeing all the house churches in Ephesus—appointing elders, addressing false teachings, and ensuring that problems are dealt with before they spread. In the first seven verses of chapter two, Paul addressed the importance of prayer for all people, including kings and those in authority, that believers might live quiet and peaceable lives in all godliness. Now Paul turns to apply these principles more specifically.

Men Leading in Prayer

> *"I desire therefore that the men pray everywhere, lifting up holy hands, without wrath and doubting." (1 Timothy 2:8)*

When Paul expresses a desire, it carries the weight of a command. He is addressing the men specifically—not using the generic word for mankind, but the word for males. Paul desires that men everywhere would lead in prayer. This entire section, spanning a chapter and a half, exhorts men to step up and be spiritual leaders—to lead prayer in their homes, in The Church, and everywhere.

The phrase "lifting up holy hands" may bring to mind worship services where people raise their hands in praise, and that connection is valid. But there is something deeper here. The word "holy" in this verse is *hosios* (ὅσιος), which appears only eight times in the New Testament. This is not the common word for holy, *hagios* (ἅγιος), which occurs 229 times and means "set apart." Rather, *hosios* specifically means "undefiled by sin." Paul wants men to be spiritual

27

leaders—but spiritual leaders with clean hands. As David said, "Who may ascend into the hill of the LORD? Or who may stand in His holy place? He who has clean hands and a pure heart..." (Psalm 24:3-4) Men should not be hypocrites but should actually have clean hands when they lift them up to the Lord in prayer.

Paul adds that this should be done "without wrath and doubting." Men are to lead with godly character, free from ungodly behaviors. Step up and be godly men. Be leaders.

Women's Adornment

> *"In like manner also, that the women adorn themselves in modest apparel, with propriety and moderation, not with braided hair or gold or pearls or costly clothing, but, which is proper for women professing godliness, with good works." (1 Timothy 2:9-10)*

Just as men are to have holy hands, women are to have holy attire. Scripture is filled with principles that believers live by and examples of how those principles can be applied. Here the principle is that women should adorn themselves in modest apparel. First Peter 3 provides a parallel, where Peter exhorts women to focus on inward beauty rather than getting caught up in outward appearance.

This passage is not banning braided hair, gold, or pearls. Paul is describing a problem that was occurring—women arriving at church dressed extravagantly, drawing attention to themselves. Tertullian, the early church father, made the point that when going to church, one should not be dressed as if going to a ball. Dressing elegantly for the opera may be appropriate, but when coming to church, the focus should not be on elaborate attire that draws attention. God is not concerned about the clothing itself; He is concerned about the heart that the clothing reveals.

> *"Because the daughters of Zion are haughty,*
> *and walk with outstretched necks and*
> *wanton eyes, walking and mincing as they*
> *go, making a jingling with their feet..."*
> *(Isaiah 3:16)*

God does not care about jingles. He cares about the haughtiness, the attitude, the wantonness. In the verses that follow in Isaiah 3:18-23, God says He will take away all their finery—the anklets, scarves, crescents, pendants, veils, headdresses, perfume boxes, garments, purses, and mirrors. These items are not banned; the point is that the women of Israel at that time were so caught up in themselves that God would strip it all away. The principle remains: outward adornment sends an outward message about an inward state. What people wear sometimes communicates something about their hearts.

I have attended churches with many former German Baptists and have numerous friends who are currently German Baptists. Their distinctive dress—homemade dresses with white bonnets for the women, plain clothes with buttons for the men—was originally chosen so they would blend in with everyone else. A modest dress, a modest outfit. But now, ironically, they stick out. We have often joked about this together, lightheartedly, between good friends. Many of them are willing to confess the irony: what was designed to help them blend in now makes them stand out and be instantly recognizable.

This illustrates a crucial point: Scripture gives culturally contextual examples of biblical principles. Consider another example from 1 Corinthians 11:5: "But every woman who prays or prophesies with her head uncovered

29

dishonors her head, for that is one and the same as if her head were shaved." In Corinth, head coverings were a significant cultural marker. A married woman wearing a head covering symbolized that she was under her husband's authority. To go without one made the statement: "I am not under my husband." Paul clarifies in verse 16: "But if anyone seems to be contentious, we have no such custom, nor do the churches of God." The principle issue was about headship, not about the head covering itself, which was the cultural example.

The same applies to the holy kiss mentioned in 1 Corinthians 16:20. In their culture, greeting with a kiss was normal and hospitable. In most Western cultures today, it is not. The principle is to be friendly and hospitable; the application varies by culture. When Paul tells women to dress modestly, he is giving a timeless principle with culturally relevant examples. Wedding rings serve a similar function today—they publicly communicate marital status, much like head coverings did in Corinth.

Let a Woman Learn

> *"Let a woman learn in silence with all submission. And I do not permit a woman to teach or to have authority over a man, but to be in silence." (1 Timothy 2:11-12)*

These two verses are heavily contested, but careful examination of the Greek reveals their meaning clearly. First, notice that Paul shifts from the plural ("women" in the previous verses) to the singular ("a woman"). This is emphatic—he is pinning down the instruction to make it unmistakably clear.

It is also worth noting that Paul says "let a woman *learn*." This was revolutionary. The Jerusalem Talmud contains statements like "Women's wisdom is solely in the spindle" and "The words of the Torah should be burned rather than entrusted to a woman." That was the cultural backdrop. For Paul to say that women should learn—that they should be engaged and involved in The Church, sitting under doctrine and being taught alongside everyone else—was radical for its time.

In Silence

The word "silence" is *hēsuchia* (ἡσυχία), meaning quietness or peaceableness. It describes "the life of one who stays at home doing his own work and does not officiously meddle in the affairs of others." This same word appears in verse 2, where Paul says believers should pray for authorities "that we may lead a quiet and peaceable life." In 2 Thessalonians 3:11-12, Paul contrasts those who "walk in a disorderly manner, not working at all, but are busybodies" with the command to "work in quietness and eat their own bread." The word describes the opposite of being disorderly.

This is not saying women can never make any sound. It means they should be peaceable and not disorderly. If Paul intended complete, literal silence, he would have used *sigaō* (σιγάω), which appears nine times in the New Testament. Three of those occurrences are in 1 Corinthians 14, where Paul instructs that if there is no interpreter for tongues, the speaker should "keep silent" (14:28); that prophets should "keep silent" while another is speaking (14:30); and that women should "keep silent in the churches" (14:34).

How do these instructions harmonize? Context is key. First Corinthians 14 addresses order in The Church service. The command for silence regarding tongues, prophecy, and

31

women asking questions all relate to maintaining orderly worship. But 1 Corinthians 11:5 already established that women prayed and prophesied aloud in The Church—they just needed to have their heads covered when doing so. Complete silence in every context was never the expectation.

With All Submission

"Submission" is *hupotagē* (ὑποταγή), from the verb *hupotassō* (ὑποτάσσω). This is a military term meaning to arrange oneself under authority. It describes "a voluntary attitude of giving in, cooperating, assuming responsibility, carrying a burden." The word breaks down to *hupo* (under) and *tassō* (to arrange). Christians are told to be in submission to the gospel. Children are told to be in submission to their parents. Wives are told to submit to their husbands in Ephesians 5.

A helpful distinction exists between submission and subjection. Submission is illustrated beautifully in *The Lord of the Rings: The Fellowship of the Ring* (2001), when the dying Boromir says to Aragorn: "I would have followed you, my brother, my captain, my king." That is willing submission to recognized authority. Subjection, by contrast, is illustrated in *Superman II* (1980), with: "Son of Jor-El, kneel before Zod!" That is forced obedience by power. There is no subjection in The Church—whether from a pastor to the congregation or from women to men. It is always to be willing submission. As a summary: submission is the act of willingly yielding to a recognized authority, while subjection is the act of forcing obedience by power.

Not to Teach or Have Authority

Paul continues: "I do not permit a woman to teach or to have authority over a man." The word "teach" uses the present tense in Greek, which typically indicates ongoing action—being a teacher, rather than teaching on any single occasion. If Paul had used the aorist tense, it would mean "never teach on any occasion, ever." Instead, the present tense suggests that women were not to be among the regular teachers of The Church—those with ongoing teaching authority.

Ephesians 4:11 identifies the offices Christ gave to The Church: apostles, prophets, evangelists, and pastor-teachers. Grammatically (by the Granville Sharp rule), "pastors and teachers" form one combined role. The teachers of The Church are the pastors—those with authority who do the regular teaching. Paul is saying women should not occupy that role.

The phrase "have authority" translates *authenteō* (αὐθεντέω), which appears only here in the New Testament. Some argue over its precise meaning, but extensive research confirms it means "to exercise authority, to govern, to exercise dominion over." For those wanting to explore this further, Andreas Köstenberger and Thomas Schreiner's book *Women in the Church* dedicates 365 pages to examining 1 Timothy 2:12, walking through hundreds of years of ancient Greek documents showing how this word was used.

Verses 11 and 12 form a deliberate contrast. Women are told *to learn* but *not to teach*. They are to be *in quietness* rather than doing *vocal teaching*. They are to have *submission* rather than *authority*. These contrasts clarify Paul's meaning.

It is important to remember that these commands apply within The Church and the home—not everywhere in the world. Galatians 3:28 declares: "There is neither Jew nor Greek, there is neither slave nor free, there is neither male nor female; for you are all one in Christ Jesus." In terms of position before Christ, all are equal. Everyone receives salvation on an equal basis. Everyone will be judged equally. But this does not negate the gender distinctions God designed. There were still slaves and free, still men and women, with distinct roles in certain contexts.

The Complementarian-Egalitarian Spectrum

Two primary views exist on this topic: the complementarian view and the egalitarian view. These are not simply two camps but represent a spectrum, with people holding positions closer to the middle or closer to the extremes.

The egalitarian position holds that men and women should have no distinctions—whether in the home or The Church, all roles are equally open to both. The complementarian position holds that God made men and women different and designed them to complement each other, with some role distinctions in the home and church.

Mike Winger, in his extensive video series on Women in Ministry (totaling over fifty hours of teaching), describes himself as a "soft complementarian." That description fits my own position as well. Winger states from the outset that he simply wants to believe the Bible—if Scripture teaches something, that is what he will believe, even if it is uncomfortable. I share that commitment.

I have fellowshipped with Christians who do not allow women to speak at all in The Church—not even during breaks. When challenged about 1 Corinthians 11, where women clearly pray and prophesy in the assembly, they offer unconvincing explanations. That represents an extreme position. On the other end, some are adamant that women can and should be pastors.

Like many people who support women pastors, I was raised under a woman pastor as a child and never thought it was a problem—until I was taken to the Scripture and had to determine what God desired. I still have coffee regularly with a local woman pastor. We have great conversations, and I encourage her in her ministry. There are some things that I am willing to disagree about, yet still attempt to maintain unity within the Body of Christ. I disagree with some Pentecostals about how they handle the gift of tongues. Yet, I also disagree with other churches about their denial of the gifts of the Spirit. Disagreement does not prevent friendship, fellowship, or ministry together. There are absolutely issues we cannot disagree on (Salvation by grace through faith, the deity of Jesus Christ, His death and resurrection, etc.,) but we can agree to disagree on many issues that divide denominations. And when asked what I truly believe, I will give an honest answer.

Common Arguments Addressed

"The women in Ephesus were uneducated."

Some argue this was merely a local problem for that time. But was there truly not a single educated woman in all of Ephesus? That is historically implausible. And what about uneducated men? If education were the issue, Paul would have established an educational standard—which he does in chapter 3, requiring that leaders be "able to teach" and "not a novice." Furthermore, we know Priscilla was in Ephesus. When Paul left Corinth for Ephesus in Acts 18, he brought Priscilla and Aquila with him. Priscilla and Aquila taught Apollos "the way of God more accurately" (Acts 18:26)—a woman instructing a man, though in a private setting, not from the pulpit. In 2 Timothy, written over a decade later, Paul greets Priscilla and Aquila—they are still in Ephesus. Priscilla was an educated, godly woman who knew the Word of God. Yet Paul says, "I do not permit a woman to teach." Education is not the issue.

"This was because of the Temple of Artemis and Diana worship."

The temple of Diana (Artemis) in Ephesus was one of the Seven Wonders of the Ancient World. But pagan worship in Ephesus was no different from pagan worship in Corinth, Rome, Athens, or any other major Greek city. If these instructions only applied to Ephesus because of local circumstances, what else would be discarded? Second Timothy is also written to Timothy in Ephesus—would that be thrown out? The book of Ephesians was written to Ephesus—what from that letter no longer applies? Jesus addressed a letter to Ephesus in Revelation 2—is that also culturally limited? This is a slippery slope. When head coverings are discussed in 1 Corinthians 11, Paul explicitly identifies them as a custom: "We have no such custom." The Bible itself tells us when something is culturally bound. Paul gives no such indication here.

"If women can prophesy, why can't they teach?"

Philip had four daughters who prophesied (Acts 21:9). Women in Corinth prophesied with heads covered (1 Corinthians 11:5). But prophecy and teaching are very different. Teaching is planned, prepared, and delivered by a person in authority. Prophecy is spontaneous—a move of the Holy Spirit that cannot be scheduled. Prophecy is for edification, exhortation, and comfort (1 Corinthians 14:3; Acts 15:32). Furthermore, prophecy is subject to scrutiny: "Let two or three prophets speak, and let the others judge" (1 Corinthians 14:29). Teaching from the pulpit does not normally involve the congregation judging whether the teacher spoke accurately. (Though this isn't discouraging being Bereans.) These are distinct gifts with different functions.

"What about Deborah? She was a judge over Israel."

Indeed she was. Israel also had queens—Athaliah ruled as queen, even if infamously. But 1 Timothy 3:15 provides the key: "I write so that you may know how you ought to conduct yourself in the house of God." These instructions are for The Church. Nothing in Scripture prohibits women from being presidents, business owners, or leaders in the secular world. Outside The Church, these rules do not apply. Deborah was a judge, but she was never a priest. The priesthood was restricted to descendants of Aaron from the tribe of Levi. Moses could not enter the tabernacle's Holy Place. David could not. The prophets could not—unless they were also priests. Being the spiritual leader of God's people has never been open to everyone.

"Aren't we all equal in Christ?"

Yes—Galatians 3:28 affirms this. But consider: if "there is neither male nor female" eliminates all role distinctions, the same logic opens the door to transgenderism, same-sex relationships, and much more. If there is truly no distinction between male and female, who can say two men cannot marry? Who can say a man cannot become a woman? Again, it is a slippery slope.

"It isn't fair."

King Uzziah was a good and godly king who loved the Lord and did great things for Israel. But in 2 Chronicles 26:16-23, he entered the temple to burn incense, and God struck him with leprosy. Why? Because he was not a priest. If someone was not a descendant of Aaron, they could not enter the temple to perform priestly duties. Was that fair? Well, it was God's choice. God selected the Levites to serve around the temple, and from among them, Aaron's descendants to serve as priests. Fairness is not the standard; God's design is.

Why: Creation and the Fall

> *"For Adam was formed first, then Eve. And Adam was not deceived, but the woman being deceived, fell into transgression."*
> *(1 Timothy 2:13-14)*

Paul now gives his reasons—and they have nothing to do with local Ephesian culture. He appeals to creation and the fall. This would have been the perfect opportunity for Paul to say, "Because of Diana worship," or "Because of a lack of education," or "Because of your unique circumstances in Ephesus." Instead, he says, "Because Adam and Eve."

First, the creative order: Adam was formed first, then Eve. Genesis 2:18 records: "And the LORD God said, 'It is not good that man should be alone; I will make him a helper comparable to him.'" First Corinthians 11:3 states: "But I want you to know that the head of every man is Christ, the head of woman is man, and the head of Christ is God." The Trinity provides a model—the Son is co-equal with the Father in every way, yet there is an order of submission. First Corinthians 11:8-9 adds: "For man is not from woman, but woman from man. Nor was man created for the woman, but woman for the man."

Why is this order built into creation? Ephesians 5:23 explains: "For the husband is head of the wife, as also Christ is head of The Church." And Ephesians 5:32: "This is a great mystery, but I speak concerning Christ and The Church." From the beginning, God made men and women different, complementary, so that in marriage—when two become one—there would be a picture of Christ and His church. The wife's submission pictures The Church submitting to Christ. The husband's sacrificial love pictures Christ laying down His life for His bride. This picture only matters in two places: the home and The Church. That is why these instructions apply specifically in God's house and in believers' houses. God wants men to step up, to be spiritual leaders, to lead their homes in prayer and godliness.

Second, the fall: "Adam was not deceived, but the woman being deceived, fell into transgression." Curses came with the fall. For the man: "Cursed is the ground for your sake; in toil you shall eat of it all the days of your life. Both thorns and thistles it shall bring forth for you... In the sweat of your face you shall eat bread" (Genesis 3:17-19). God made men strong because they would have to work hard to provide for their families. For the woman: "I will greatly multiply your sorrow and your conception; in pain you shall bring forth children; your desire shall be for your husband, and he shall rule over you" (Genesis 3:16). Part of the curse established an order in the home.

I once had to discipline my son for hitting his sister. I read Genesis 3 with him and explained: "God made you a man. He made you strong because you are supposed to be strong for your wife someday. When God cursed the ground, He told Adam it would not be easy to make a living—you will

39

have to sweat for it. God made you able to bear that burden so you could lead and love your wife. Right now, your sisters are your practice. You are to protect them, watch out for them, look over them, and provide for them." The curse brought difficulty, but also defined roles.

Whenever people argue that these instructions were only for that time and place, Paul's appeal to creation provides the most sweeping context possible. These verses may be harder to swallow for modern sensibilities, but they are actually straightforward to teach because the text is clear.

Saved in Childbearing

"Nevertheless she will be saved in childbearing if they continue in faith, love, and holiness, with self-control."
(1 Timothy 2:15)

This verse has generated many interpretations. Two historically common but problematic interpretations should be set aside. First, that women receive spiritual salvation by having babies—this contradicts salvation by grace alone through faith alone. Second, that women will be physically protected during childbirth if they continue in faith—this simply does not match reality, as godly women have died in childbirth throughout history.

Two better interpretations exist. Some suggest that women are eternally saved "through the childbearing"—that is, through bringing forth the Messiah. Since Paul just referenced the Garden of Eden, this view has some merit. But the most satisfying interpretation understands "saved" not as eternal salvation but as experiencing the fullness of salvation. Philippians 2:12 uses similar language: "Work out your own salvation with fear and trembling." This does not mean working for eternal salvation but experiencing the fruit and fullness of what salvation provides—peace, hope, love, joy, and purpose.

Duane Litfin writes in *The Bible Knowledge Commentary*: "A woman will find her greatest satisfaction and meaning in life, not in seeking the male role, but in fulfilling God's design for her as wife and mother with all 'faith, love, and holiness, with self-control.'" This makes excellent sense. Despite the curse that brought pain to childbirth, a woman will experience the fullness of her salvation by embracing her unique calling—a calling men cannot fulfill, since men cannot bear children.

The poem by William Ross Wallace captures it well: "The hand that rocks the cradle is the hand that rules the world." Where would the world be without Susanna Wesley, mother of Charles and John Wesley? Godly women have shaped history by raising godly children. Paul is saying that God made women for a reason. Rather than striving to be something God did not design them to be, women should embrace their calling and experience the fullness of what God has planned.

What About Exceptions?

Can women ever speak from the pulpit? There are reasonable exceptions to consider.

Testimonies: Many women have shared their testimonies in church. This is not the same as teaching with authority. A new believer—whether man or woman—would not be asked to deliver a sermon, but any believer might be invited to share what God has done in their life.

Missionaries: Female missionaries have gone to places where no Christian men exist. What are they supposed to do? Gladys Aylward in China is a classic example.

41

Someone had to teach, and for a season, she was the only option.

Special events and circumstances: Corrie ten Boom attended Calvary Chapel Costa Mesa in her later years. Pastor Chuck Smith gave her the pulpit to share her remarkable story. No one thought she was the pastor or was teaching with pastoral authority—she was sharing a powerful testimony that everyone needed to hear.

During the COVID-19 pandemic, a pastor friend at a neighboring church discovered that the Washington state attorney for the Pacific Justice Institute attended his church and served in the children's ministry. He brought her up to explain legalities and answer questions. When expert knowledge is needed, and the expert happens to be a woman, that is a reasonable circumstance.

What about titles like "Women's Ministry Pastor" or "Kids Ministry Pastor"? Women are exhorted to teach other women and to teach children. Technically, if a woman's role involves only women or children, there may be no conflict—she is not exercising authority over men. Practically, however, titles can create confusion. A friend of mine, who I like to tease and call "Prophet Mitch," is an assisting pastor at a neighboring church with an extraordinary gift in counseling. I joke with him about the title "Prophet" because he resists it—and for good reason. Titles carry assumptions and can confuse people. In a day when there is already confusion about women pastors, unnecessary titles may only add to it. The solution is not to eliminate women from ministry but to be thoughtful about how roles are described. Women oversee women's ministry, children's ministry, finances, worship, and many other areas in healthy churches. The restriction is specifically on the role of pastor-elder-overseer—the one who teaches with authority over the congregation.

Qualifications for Overseers

Paul addresses women in leadership because he is about to discuss leadership in The Church. The early church had various leadership roles: apostles, prophets, bishops, pastors, elders, and deacons. Understanding these distinctions is helpful.

Ephesians 2:20 describes The Church as "built on the foundation of the apostles and prophets, Jesus Christ Himself being the chief cornerstone." For the first seventy years, The Church had living apostles—eyewitnesses of Jesus Christ and His teachings. They held a unique and foundational role. When reading the early church fathers, the title "apostle" disappeared after that generation; they did not call the next leaders apostles. The apostles were those whom Jesus Christ personally appointed.

After the apostles, bishops emerged to oversee multiple churches—similar to Timothy's role overseeing numerous house churches in Ephesus. But the "bishop" in 1 Timothy 3:1 is likely not this kind of regional overseer. The word is *episkopē* (ἐπισκοπή), comes from *epi* (over, upon) and *skopos* (to watch, observe)—literally, "overseer." This is where the term "Episcopalian" originates. "Overseer" is a better translation than "bishop," which carries later ecclesiastical connotations.

Ephesians 4:11 mentions "pastors and teachers" as one combined role (by the Granville Sharp rule in Greek grammar). The pastor-teacher filled a primary teaching role in local congregations. Biblically, pastors and elders are essentially the same thing. In Acts 20:17, Paul "sent to Ephesus and called for the elders of The Church." In verse 28, he tells these same elders: "Therefore take heed to yourselves and to all the flock, among which the Holy Spirit has made you overseers [*episkopous*], to shepherd [*poimainō*—the verb form of "pastor"] The Church of God." Paul gathers the elders, calls them overseers, and tells them to pastor. These terms describe the same role.

Some conclude from Acts 20 that churches should be led by a group of elders. But The Church in Ephesus was not one large congregation—it was composed of numerous house churches. When Paul calls for "the elders of Ephesus," he is gathering the leaders of many individual congregations. Each elder pastored his own church.

How large was The Church in Ephesus? Acts 19:19 records that converts brought their magic books to be burned, and "they counted up the value of them, and it totaled fifty thousand pieces of silver." That is 50,000 denarii—50,000 days' wages for a laborer. Using a modern equivalent of an $18 per hour wage, for eight hours a day, that equals $7,200,000 worth of books! If each person brought $500 worth of books, that represents 14,400 people. If each brought $100 worth, that represents 72,000 people. Even conservative estimates suggest there were thousands of believers in Ephesus. By Acts 4:4, The Church in Jerusalem already had 5,000 members. The "elders" in Ephesus were numerous because they each oversaw individual house churches throughout the city.

> *"This is a faithful saying: If a man desires the position of a bishop, he desires a good work." (1 Timothy 3:1)*

It is a good desire to want to be used by God at the highest level. The qualifications in verses 1-7 represent the highest calling for a Christian—not merely what it takes to be a good Christian, but the above-and-beyond standard. Every believer should strive for these qualities, even if God has not called them to be an elder. Being qualified, even without the title, is a worthy goal.

I once told my pastor that I felt God wasn't calling me to be a pastor but to be a highly qualified elder—that was my aim. Then God changed things and called me to be a pastor after all. Be careful what you aim for; God may have bigger plans.

Blameless

> *"A bishop then must be blameless..."*
> *(1 Timothy 3:2)*

"Blameless" is *anepilēmptos* (ἀνεπίλημπτος). Breaking down the word: *a* (the alpha privative, negating what follows), *epi* (upon), and *lambanō* (to receive). Literally: "one upon whom nothing can be received"—nothing sticks (You might call him"the Teflon man") The leader should be someone against whom no legitimate accusation can be made.

Husband of One Wife

"Husband of one wife" is literally "a one-woman man" in Greek. Greek has no separate words for husband and wife—only "man" and "woman," with marriage implied by context. Several incorrect views should be avoided: that leaders must be "married to The Church" (the Roman Catholic interpretation); that leaders must be married; that widowers cannot remarry; that this merely prohibits polygamy; or that anyone who has ever been divorced is permanently disqualified.

The phrase describes character: a man devoted to his wife, faithful, not a wanderer. Can leaders be divorced? First, actions taken as an unbeliever should generally be forgiven and not disqualify someone. What about divorce as a believer? First Corinthians 7:10-11 instructs: "A wife is not to depart from her husband. But even if she does depart, let her remain unmarried or be reconciled to her husband." When a believer unlawfully leaves a spouse, they should remain single or reconcile.

What constitutes a lawful divorce? Scripture identifies adultery (Matthew 5:32) and abandonment by an unbeliever (1 Corinthians 7:15). Paul adds, "A brother or a sister is not under bondage in such cases. But God has called us to peace." The phrase "not under bondage" suggests freedom to remarry, and "such cases" implies there may be other situations as well.

For situations that are not clear-cut, the best counsel is not to make that determination alone but to entrust it to church leadership. Jesus said in Matthew 18:18-20: "Whatever you bind on earth will be bound in heaven, and whatever you loose on earth will be loosed in heaven. Again I say to you that if two of you agree on earth concerning anything that they ask, it will be done for them by My Father in heaven." In context, this addresses disputes and discipline in The Church. When church leaders come together, examine a situation from every angle, pray, and reach agreement, Christ gives assurance that their judgment has His approval. Submitting to that kind of accountability is wise.

As a summary: an unlawful divorce should be made right if possible. If it cannot be made right, the situation should be entrusted to church leadership. Any divorce while currently in a leadership role would most likely require temporarily stepping down so the elders can examine what happened. Otherwise, a lawful divorce, reviewed by church leaders, should not be considered disqualifying for leadership.

Character Qualities

The list in verses 2-3 is primarily about character: temperate, sober-minded, of good behavior, hospitable,

able to teach, not given to wine, not violent, not greedy for money, gentle, not quarrelsome, not covetous. Depending on how the list is broken down, there are roughly fifteen qualities—and all but one are matters of character. The one exception is "able to teach," which is a spiritual gift.

This should encourage men aspiring to leadership: focus on character above all. Study and learn, yes—but the emphasis is on who a man is, not merely what he knows. The ability to teach is listed as a gift of the Spirit in 1 Corinthians 12. Interestingly, "able to teach" (*didaktikos*, διδακτικός) appears only twice in the New Testament—here and in 2 Timothy 2:24: "A servant of the Lord must not quarrel but be gentle to all, able to teach, patient." All servants of the Lord are called to be able to teach because all disciples learn in order to teach others.

Not Given to Wine

"Not given to wine" is *paroinos* (πάροινος), literally "beside wine"—historically a term for "a drinker." For elders: "not given to wine." For deacons (verse 8): "not given to much wine." For all Christians: never get drunk (Ephesians 5:18). A narrowing occurs toward the top. Christians are not to be drunk. Deacons should not be given to much wine. Elders should not be given to wine at all.

Does this require total abstinence? Many interpret it that way, and that is why I personally do not drink. The text may not explicitly require total abstinence, but it leans strongly in that direction. For a leader, it is an easy choice: avoid confusion, avoid accusation, avoid causing others to stumble. There is much to gain and little to lose.

It is worth noting that ancient wine had roughly half the alcohol content of modern wine and was typically mixed with water at ratios of 2:1 or 3:1. One glass of modern wine contains about the same alcohol as six to eight glasses of ancient wine. The cultural context was quite different.

Rules His House Well

> *"One who rules his own house well, having his children in submission with all reverence—for if a man does not know how to rule his own house, how will he take care of The Church of God?" (1 Timothy 3:4-5)*

"Rule" is *proïstēmi* (προΐστημι), meaning "to set before," to superintend, preside over, be a protector or guardian, to care for and give attention to. The principle is ruling the household well. Having children in submission is the example.

The standard is the principle, not the example. Don McClure once shared that his son was dealing drugs as a teenager. Don met the mayor, the judge, and the chief of police—all because of his son's troubles. He gave his son an ultimatum: "You can live under my authority, or you can leave." His teenage son chose to leave. As he walked out the door, Don said, "If you find anything out there better than Jesus, you come back and let me know." Six months later, his son returned and told his mother, "Tell Dad there's nothing out here better than Jesus." He eventually came around.

Don wanted to step down from leadership, but his elders said, "From everything we can see, you ruled your house well. You gave an ultimatum, you did the hard thing, and your son is a free moral agent." The best parents can have children who still go astray. The question is not whether children turn out perfectly but whether the father is dealing with issues or ignoring them, ruling well or brushing things under the rug.

48

Not a Novice

> *"...not a novice, lest being puffed up with*
> *pride he fall into the same condemnation as*
> *the devil." (1 Timothy 3:6)*

A new believer elevated too quickly becomes proud—and pride is what caused Satan's fall. Leaders need time to mature.

Good Testimony with Outsiders

> *"Moreover he must have a good testimony*
> *among those who are outside, lest he fall*
> *into reproach and the snare of the devil."*
> *(1 Timothy 3:7)*

Those outside The Church are watching. If a leader has skeletons in the closet, Satan will set traps using what outsiders know or say. A good reputation protects against reproach and snares.

Qualifications for Deacons

Acts 6 provides the origin of the deacon role. The apostles said, "It is not desirable that we should leave the word of God and serve tables. Therefore, brethren, seek out from among you seven men of good reputation, full of the Holy Spirit and wisdom, whom we may appoint over this business; but we will give ourselves continually to prayer and to the ministry of the word" (Acts 6:2-4).

Elders oversee the spiritual needs of The Church; deacons oversee the physical needs. Deacons are not a minor role—they hold positions of importance and oversight, serving under the authority of the elders. The word "deacon" (*diakonos*, διάκονος) means "servant," but in this context it refers to a specific serving role with responsibility and authority over certain ministries.

> *"Likewise deacons must be reverent, not double-tongued, not given to much wine, not greedy for money, holding the mystery of the faith with a pure conscience. But let these also first be tested; then let them serve as deacons, being found blameless."*
> *(1 Timothy 3:8-10)*

"Likewise" indicates the list is similar to the elder qualifications. Deacons must be reverent, not double-tongued ("saying what they mean, and meaning what they say"), not given to much wine, not greedy, holding the faith with a pure conscience. Verse 10 adds that they should "first be tested"—people are worked into leadership, not placed at the top immediately. Faithfulness in smaller roles leads to greater responsibility.

My own progression illustrates this. When I had been attending church for a while, I was asked to be a greeter. Layer I was asked to help with the midweek children's ministry. Next I joined the worship team. One summer I was asked to teach a small devotional as we met in the park, then a full evening service, and eventually at a Sunday morning service. Over time I got asked to be an elder, and then I came to find out that God wanted me to be a pastor. Each step tested faithfulness before the next door opened. For those who desire leadership, the path begins with serving wherever a door opens and serving there faithfully.

Women Deacons

"Likewise, their wives must be reverent, not
slanderers, temperate, faithful in all things."
(1 Timothy 3:11)

The New King James translation does a disservice to this
verse. It would be odd for deacons to be qualified by their
wives while elders are not. Furthermore, the Greek does not
actually say "their wives"—it literally just says "the
women" (*gunaikas*). Greek has no separate word for
"wife"; the word for "woman" is used, and marriage is
implied by context. Notice that verse 8 begins with
"Likewise" introducing the deacons, and verse 11 begins
with "Likewise" introducing these women. The structure
suggests Paul is addressing women who serve as deacons—
or "deaconesses".

The New Testament includes examples of women serving
in such roles. Phoebe is called a *diakonos* in Romans 16:1
and delivered Paul's letter to the Romans, just as Tychicus
delivered the letters to Ephesus, Colossae, and Philemon.
Women in the early church had many significant roles—it
was only the role of pastor-elder that was restricted to men.

Some complementarians take things too far by missing the
biblical examples of women serving in The Church.
Women may oversee children's ministry, finances, worship,
and various other ministries. These are deaconess-type
roles—not just serving but overseeing and taking
responsibility for a ministry. The qualifications apply:
reverent, not slanderers, temperate, faithful in all things.

"Let deacons be the husbands of one wife,
ruling their children and their own houses
well. For those who have served well as
deacons obtain for themselves a good
standing and great boldness in the faith

51

which is in Christ Jesus."
(1 Timothy 3:12-13)

The same standard regarding marriage and household
management applies to deacons as to elders. And the
reward for faithful service is significant: good standing and
great boldness in the faith. Not everyone will be an elder,
but there is always room for more deacons. Faithful service
as a deacon often leads to other ministries and greater
opportunities. Philip, one of the original seven from Acts 6,
became Philip the evangelist. Stephen, another of the
seven, became the first Christian martyr while preaching
and seeing many people saved. Many who begin serving as
deacons eventually move into other places of prominence
and ministry.

The Purpose of These Instructions

"These things I write to you, though I hope
to come to you shortly; but if I am delayed, I
write so that you may know how you ought
to conduct yourself in the house of God,
which is The Church of the living God, the
pillar and ground of the truth."
(1 Timothy 3:14-15)

This is the purpose statement for everything Paul has
written. He wants Timothy—and through him, all
believers—to know how to conduct themselves in the
house of God. The Church is not merely a human
institution; it is The Church of the living God, the pillar and
ground of the truth. How The Church orders itself matters.
How believers conduct themselves in God's house matters.
These instructions about men leading in prayer, women
adorning themselves with modesty and good works,
learning with submission, the qualifications for elders and

deacons—all of it serves the purpose of right conduct in God's household.

May God raise up more people to serve—men stepping up as spiritual leaders, women embracing their vital roles, qualified elders shepherding the flock, and faithful deacons meeting the physical needs of The Church. There are always opportunities for God to use people, new ministries to launch, and needs to meet. The Church needs servants who will not just show up but own their ministries and care for the people. That is what leadership in God's house looks like.

The Pastoral Epistles

The Mystery of Godliness
1 Timothy 3:16

[Note: This brief chapter was originally taught on Christmas Day, which accounts for its seasonal reflections on the incarnation.]

In the previous chapter, Paul covered church government—the roles of men and women, the qualifications for elders and deacons, and how believers ought to conduct themselves in the house of God. It is all very clear, instructional teaching. Then, at the end of chapter 3, something shifts. A poetic piece appears:

> *"And without controversy great is the mystery of godliness: God was manifested in the flesh, justified in the Spirit, seen by angels, preached among the Gentiles, believed on in the world, received up in glory." (1 Timothy 3:16)*

An Ancient Hymn

The Christian faith has always been a musical faith. From the Psalms in the Old Testament to the earliest days of the Church, believers have sung about what they believe. Colossians 3:16 instructs: "Let the word of Christ dwell in you richly in all wisdom, teaching and admonishing one another in psalms and hymns and spiritual songs, singing with grace in your hearts to the Lord." Singing is not merely for worship and getting hearts in the right place—it is also a way believers learn. Before the printing press, before Gutenberg, people did not have ready access to books. They sang, and through singing they memorized and internalized truth.

Even in the Gospels, at the end of the Last Supper, Jesus and His disciples "sang a hymn" before going out to the Mount of Olives where Jesus would be arrested (Matthew 26:30). Hymns have always been part of the faith.

Scholars have identified several markers that help recognize when a New Testament writer may be quoting an early Christian hymn:

Contextual dislocation: The passage seems almost out of place. The writer is teaching one thing, and suddenly something poetic appears that feels different from the surrounding material. Often this is because the writer is quoting words his readers already knew—familiar lyrics that did not need introduction.

Change of style: Straightforward instruction gives way to poetic structure. First Timothy 2 and 3 consist of clear, direct teaching about church order. Then verse 16 arrives with its rhythmic, balanced lines.

Introductory phrase: Hymns often come with a phrase that sets them apart, signaling that a quotation follows.

Parallels and contrasts: Poetry thrives on contrasting ideas and parallel structures—exactly what appears in this verse.

Rare vocabulary: Hymns frequently use unusual words. The introductory word in 1 Timothy 3:16 appears nowhere else in the entire Bible.

Another likely example of an early church hymn appears in Ephesians 5:14: "Therefore He says: 'Awake, you who sleep, arise from the dead, and Christ will give you light.'" This is not a quotation from the Old Testament. Most scholars believe Paul is citing a chorus sung in the early church—a short, memorable piece repeated in worship. The same appears to be true of 1 Timothy 3:16.

Without Controversy

The phrase "without controversy" translates a single Greek word: *homologoumenōs* (ὁμολογουμένως). This word appears only here in the entire New Testament—exactly the kind of rare vocabulary that often marks a hymn. Breaking down the word reveals its meaning:

Homo means "the same." *Logeō* (from *logos*) means "to speak." Together they form *homologeō*—"to confess," literally "to speak the same thing." Biblical confession is not merely pouring out secrets; it is agreeing with God. God calls something sin; the believer confesses by agreeing—speaking the same thing. God says salvation comes through Jesus; the believer confesses by agreeing.

The ending *-menōs* comes from *menō*, meaning "to abide" or "to remain." Put together, *homologoumenōs* describes an "abiding confession"—something confessed repeatedly, an ongoing declaration that everyone recognizes and agrees upon. Paul is saying: "This is something we confess often. This is familiar. No one disagrees about this." It is an ancient creed set to music.

Great Is the Mystery of Godliness

"Great is the mystery of godliness." A mystery in Scripture is not something unknowable but something that could never be discovered without God revealing it. The existence of God is not a mystery—Romans 1 declares that creation itself testifies to God's existence. Everyone should recognize that there is a God. But there is much about God that humanity could never know unless He revealed it. The mystery of godliness encompasses the truths about who God is and what He has done—truths unveiled through His Word.

What follows is the content of this ancient confession, structured as three couplets—three pairs of contrasting lines.

Manifested in the Flesh, Justified in the Spirit

"God was manifested in the flesh." This is the incarnation—Christmas in a single phrase. Jesus spoke of it in John 6 as the bread from heaven coming down to earth. John 1 declares that the Word who was with God and was God "became flesh and dwelt among us." Philippians 2 describes how He "did not consider it robbery to be equal with God, but made Himself of no reputation, taking the form of a bondservant, and coming in the likeness of men."

This is staggering to comprehend: the eternal, all-powerful God of the universe came as a baby—a vulnerable infant who would grow up experiencing everything humans experience. Hebrews reminds believers that "we do not have a High Priest who cannot sympathize with our weaknesses, but was in all points tempted as we are, yet without sin" (Hebrews 4:15). He was "touched with our infirmities," as the older translations put it. He can relate because He lived it.

"Justified in the Spirit." If the first line is Christmas, this is Easter. It is by the Spirit that Jesus was raised from the dead. Without the resurrection, Jesus would have been just another man making claims. But when He rose from the dead, He proved He was exactly who He claimed to be. The resurrection is the vindication, the justification, the seal that confirms everything.

Seen by Angels, Preached Among the Gentiles

"Seen by angels"—or as some translations render it, "beheld by angels." Before Jesus came to earth, all of heaven knew who He was. The angelic hosts beheld Him in glory. But then He descended, and now "preached among the Gentiles"—proclaimed among the nations. The One whom angels gazed upon in heaven is now proclaimed to all peoples on earth.

This contrast highlights the expansion of God's revelation. In the Old Testament, the Jewish people—roughly 0.2% of the world's population—were the ones who had the temple, the Scriptures, and the promise of the Messiah. It was a small percentage of humanity. But after the gospel went forth, over a third of the world now identifies as Christian. From a tiny fraction to billions—He is preached among the nations.

Believed On in the World, Received Up in Glory

"Believed on in the world." The message has taken root. People have responded. Faith has spread across the globe.

"Received up in glory." The ascension—Jesus returning to the Father, taking His rightful place at the right hand of God. The One who humbled Himself to become a man, who died and rose again, has been exalted to the highest place.

An Abiding Confession

This single verse captures the sweep of redemptive history: incarnation, resurrection, angelic witness, global proclamation, worldwide faith, and glorious ascension. It is theology compressed into poetry, doctrine set to music, truth meant to be sung and remembered.

The early church sang these words. They confessed them together, again and again, until they became an abiding confession—something everyone knew, something no one disputed. "Without controversy, great is the mystery of godliness."

And so it remains. God was manifested in the flesh. He came for us. He lived among us. He died and rose again. He ascended in glory. And He is believed on throughout the world. This is the mystery of godliness—and it is great indeed.

Holding Fast in Hard Times
1 Timothy 4

This chapter is full of practical application. Paul addresses false teachers and their teachings, warns about the challenges of the latter times, and gives Timothy exhortations that every believer can embrace. The title "Holding Fast in Hard Times" captures the essence of what Paul communicates: in a world filled with deception and difficulty, believers must cling to sound doctrine and godly living.

False Teachers and Their Teachings

> *"Now the Spirit expressly says that in latter times some will depart from the faith, giving heed to deceiving spirits and doctrines of demons, speaking lies in hypocrisy, having their own conscience seared with a hot iron, forbidding to marry, and commanding to abstain from foods which God created to be received with thanksgiving by those who believe and know the truth. For every creature of God is good, and nothing is to be refused if it is received with thanksgiving; for it is sanctified by the word of God and prayer." (1 Timothy 4:1-5)*

The Holy Spirit expressly—explicitly, not merely hinting—states that in the latter times some will depart from the faith. This is late in Paul's ministry; he is writing one of his final letters. The warning echoes throughout Scripture.

61

Daniel 8:23 speaks of the end times: "In the latter time of their kingdom, when the transgressors have reached their fullness, a king shall arise, having fierce features, who understands sinister schemes." This refers to the Antichrist—a time when transgression reaches its peak. Jesus warned in Matthew 24:11-12, 24: "Then many false prophets will rise up and deceive many. And because lawlessness will abound, the love of many will grow cold... For false christs and false prophets will rise and show great signs and wonders to deceive, if possible, even the elect." Second Thessalonians 2:3 adds: "Let no one deceive you by any means; for that Day will not come unless the falling away comes first, and the man of sin is revealed, the son of perdition." This "falling away" is often called the great apostasy.

First John 2:18-19 puts it plainly: "Little children, it is the last hour; and as you have heard that the Antichrist is coming, even now many antichrists have come, by which we know that it is the last hour. They went out from us, but they were not of us; for if they had been of us, they would have continued with us; but they went out that they might be made manifest, that none of them were of us."

Departing from the Faith

Notice that Paul writes "*the* faith" with the definite article. This differs from simply "faith." Throughout Scripture, "faith" refers to personal belief—saving faith, faith for miracles, the gift of faith mentioned in 1 Corinthians 12. But "the faith" typically refers to the orthodox teachings of The Church, the collective body of Christian doctrine. Departing from "the faith" means walking away from sound teaching and The Church itself.

Unbelievers can depart from the faith by showing their true colors and walking away from a church to which they never truly belonged. This is exactly what John describes in 1 John 2:19—they went out to make manifest that they were never truly part of the body. Jesus warned of this in Matthew 7:21-23, where people cry "Lord, Lord" and claim to have done mighty works, yet Jesus responds, "I never knew you." That sounds heavy, but it is also comforting: Jesus does not say "I used to know you" but "I *never* knew you." They were never truly His.

Believers can also depart from the faith through backsliding. When believers walk away from The Church and away from God, they lose much. They lose *power*— God gives supernatural power to His people. They lose *protection*—there is supernatural protection when walking strong in faith. In 1 Corinthians 5, when Paul instructs The Church to put out an evildoer, he speaks of delivering him "to Satan for the destruction of the flesh." While that man attended The Church, he had protection; removal meant losing it. Backsliders lose *provision*, *peace*, and their *prize*—the heavenly rewards they should be storing up.

The illustration is simple: picture a lone zebra separated from the herd, with a lion prowling nearby. The lions do not attack the pack; they go after the isolated one. Someone might say, "I can be a Christian without going to church." Technically, that statement is accurate. But such a person is missing out on power, protection, provision, peace, and prize. The enemy knows isolated believers are vulnerable.

Deceiving Spirits and Doctrines of Demons

Paul warns that those departing from the faith give heed to "deceiving spirits and doctrines of demons." The phrase "doctrines of demons" grammatically means doctrines taught and inspired by demons, not doctrines *about* demons. This goes back to the Garden of Eden. Satan told Eve, "You will not surely die. For God knows that in the day you eat of it your eyes will be opened, and you will be like God, knowing good and evil" (Genesis 3:4-5). That was a doctrine of a demon—teaching something contrary to what God had said. Satan was deceiving her, and as Paul noted in chapter 2, "the woman being deceived, fell into transgression."

Demons know that getting Christians doctrinally off course will hurt them. The more false teachings someone embraces, the more concern arises about whether they are truly converted. The Holy Spirit is supposed to be the believer's teacher, guiding into all truth. If someone has the Holy Spirit, how are they getting caught up in so many false teachings? There are saved people in some doctrinally confused churches—that is certain. But demons work to pull believers as far to the fringe as possible, getting them to believe things that damage their faith.

The results of believing demonic doctrines are significant. Unbelievers are kept from saving faith—all false religion is satanic in origin, designed to lead people away from the truth. Believers are kept from bearing fruit. Satan may not be able to snatch someone from Jesus's hand, but he can certainly get them off track. Additionally, false doctrine often isolates believers, whereas true doctrine promotes unity. Those with a solid, balanced understanding of Scripture can usually coexist with people who hold some different views without making a big deal of it. But those deceived by false teachings often isolate themselves, refusing fellowship with anyone who does not share their peculiar beliefs.

Paul describes these false teachers as "speaking lies in hypocrisy, having their own conscience seared with a hot iron." The word "seared" is *kaustēriazō* (καυστηριάζω), the root of "cauterize." When a wound bleeds, a hot piece of metal can be applied to stop the bleeding—cauterization. Paul is saying their conscience has been cauterized. Anyone who has seen someone swept up in false teaching recognizes this: it is as if their logic and reason have been burned away. The brain power that should logically examine Scripture no longer flows. They are caught up in lies and believe them wholeheartedly because their conscience has been seared.

Forbidding Marriage and Foods

Paul gives two specific examples of demonic doctrines: forbidding marriage and commanding abstinence from foods. These are not the only false teachings, but they were specific to the situation Timothy faced.

Regarding marriage: the Essenes (the Jewish community at Qumran where the Dead Sea Scrolls were found) and the Therapeutae (a similar group in Alexandria, Egypt) largely banned marriage. The Gnostics were also against marriage. More recently, the celibacy of priests in the Roman Catholic Church falls into this category—it is not biblical. Peter had a wife, and the Catholic Church holds Peter in high esteem. The grammar of verse 3 actually includes both marriage and food as things "God created to be received with thanksgiving." Both were designed by God to be enjoyed.

Paul addresses the gift of celibacy in 1 Corinthians 7, explaining that some people receive this gift—they are content to remain single and serve the Lord fully. Paul himself had this gift. But just as no one chooses their spiritual gifts, no one chooses to have the gift of celibacy. It is given by God. To forbid marriage universally contradicts Scripture.

Regarding foods: the Judaizers tried to impose Old Testament dietary laws on Christians. The Gnostics also forbade certain foods. Mandatory fasts imposed by religious authorities—rather than Spirit-led, individually chosen fasting—fall into the same problematic category. When something meant to be voluntary and Spirit-led becomes imposed on others, it becomes a problem.

The Seventh-day Adventist Church provides a notable modern example. Ellen G. White, the prophetess whose writings are highly esteemed in that denomination, taught extensively against eating meat. She wrote: "Again and again I have been shown that God is trying to lead us back, step by step, to His original design—that man should subsist upon the natural products of the earth... Vegetables, fruits, and grains should compose our diet. Not an ounce of flesh meat should enter our stomachs. The eating of flesh is unnatural. We are to return to God's original purpose in the creation of man." She also wrote: "Among those who are waiting for the coming of the Lord, meat eating will eventually be done away; flesh will cease to form a part of their diet. We should ever keep this end in view, and endeavor to work steadily toward it. I cannot think that in the practice of flesh eating we are in harmony with the light which God has been pleased to give us."

But Paul writes plainly: "For every creature of God is good, and nothing is to be refused if it is received with thanksgiving; for it is sanctified by the word of God and prayer." The word "creature" (*ktisma*) means "created thing" and in Scripture typically refers to living creatures. Every creature of God is good; nothing is to be refused if received with thanksgiving. This passage, incidentally, has been used since the early church to explain why Christians pray before meals—the food is sanctified by the word of God and prayer.

A Good Minister of Jesus Christ

"If you instruct the brethren in these things, you will be a good minister of Jesus Christ, nourished in the words of faith and of the good doctrine which you have carefully followed. But reject profane and old wives' fables, and exercise yourself toward godliness." (1 Timothy 4:6-7)

The word "instruct" is *hypotithēmi* (ὑποτίθημι), meaning "to lay before" or "to set in front." It appears only twice in the New Testament. This is not aggressive, instructive teaching; it is simply laying the truth before people. When there is conflict or confusion in The Church over issues like food laws, Timothy's job is to lay Scripture before them and let them decide what to do with it. Sometimes the Spirit leads to strong rebuke, but often the approach is simply: "Here is what Scripture says. You figure it out."

By doing this, Timothy will be "a good minister of Jesus Christ, nourished in the words of faith and of the good doctrine." The key is staying close to the Word of God and the doctrines—the beliefs of The Church based on that Word. Throughout history, returning to Scripture has been either the cause or the effect of revival. In Jesus's day, the Pharisees and Sadducees were angry that He did not keep "the traditions of the fathers"—the washing of pots and similar additions to the law. Jesus replied that they followed traditions of men rather than the Word of God. The same pattern repeats through history: religion grows encrusted with traditions until someone returns to the simple teachings God actually gave. Josiah found the Law, and the people returned to what Scripture said. The Church does well to keep things simple: what the Bible says, we do; where it is silent, we exercise liberty.

Paul then tells Timothy to "reject profane and old wives' fables." The word "reject" is *paraiteomai* (παραιτέομαι). In the active voice, it means to beg, entreat, or make an excuse—trying to make something not happen. In the passive voice, as here, it means to shun, avert, refuse, or avoid. The King James translates it "refuse"; the NIV and ESV say "have nothing to do with"; the NLT says "don't waste your time." These translations paint a better picture than "reject," which sounds active, as if Timothy should confront every false teacher. Instead, the sense is: avoid it, do not get caught up in it, do not waste time on endless disputes.

Bodily Exercise and Godliness

> *"For bodily exercise profits a little, but godliness is profitable for all things, having promise of the life that now is and of that which is to come." (1 Timothy 4:8)*

The Greek literally reads "bodily exercise profits *for* a little"—there is a benefit, though small. The word "exercise" is *gymnasia* (γυμνασία), from which we get "gymnasium." Interestingly, it derives from *gymnos* (γυμνός), meaning "naked." In the ancient world, people would remove their outer garments to exercise in light underclothes—hence the connection between "naked" and "exercise." When Scripture describes someone "stripping off their clothes," like David before the ark or Saul among the prophets, they were not completely naked but down to their undergarments.

Those who dislike exercise sometimes cite this verse: "See, the Bible says it only profits a little!" True—but the Bible says hardly anything else profits at all. Physical exercise does have value; it just has limited value. It profits "for a little" in two senses: it provides only a small benefit compared to spiritual exercise, and it only profits for a little while. Exercise from years ago provides no benefit today if it has not continued. In the summertime, my church has a weekly fellowship at my house, and we often play frisbee. About halfway through the game, it becomes evident who has been exercising and who has not.

Paul is making what is called an *a fortiori* argument—from the lesser to the greater. Jesus loved these arguments. In Luke 11:13: "If you then, being evil, know how to give good gifts to your children, how much more will your heavenly Father give the Holy Spirit to those who ask Him!" In Luke 12:24: "Consider the ravens, for they neither sow nor reap, which have neither storehouse nor barn; and God feeds them. Of how much more value are you than the birds?" And Luke 12:28: "If then God so clothes the grass, which today is in the field and tomorrow is thrown into the oven, how much more will He clothe you, O you of little faith?" If this lesser thing is true, how much more the greater thing.

Paul applies this to Timothy: bodily exercise is profitable, but *how much more* is spiritual exercise profitable! Physical exercise has no eternal value and only profits temporarily. But godliness is profitable for all things, "having promise of the life that now is and of that which is to come." Understanding this changes how believers live. If physical things have such little value and eternal things have great value, priorities should reflect that reality. This does not mean neglecting physical health or never having hobbies— but it means keeping perspective and having priorities in order. God does not forbid enjoyment; He simply calls for proper perspective.

A Faithful Saying

"This is a faithful saying and worthy of all acceptance. For to this end we both labor and suffer reproach, because we trust in the living God, who is the Savior of all men, especially of those who believe. These things command and teach." (1 Timothy 4:9-11)

The phrase "this is a faithful saying" appears five times in the Pastoral Epistles, and many scholars believe it became a repeated phrase in the early church even after the New Testament was completed—a kind of formula like Jesus's "Verily, verily" or "Most assuredly." The five faithful sayings are:

- "Christ Jesus came into the world to save sinners" (1 Timothy 1:15).
- "If a man desires the position of an overseer, he desires a good work" (1 Timothy 3:1).
- "The living God is the Savior of all men, especially of those who believe" (1 Timothy 4:10).
- "If we died with Him, we shall also live with Him" (2 Timothy 2:11).
- "Those who have believed in God should be careful to maintain good works" (Titus 3:8).

Only in 1 Timothy 1:15 and 4:9 does Paul add "and worthy of all acceptance."

Paul explains that "to this end we both labor and suffer reproach." The word "labor" carries the sense of agonizing, grueling work—the root of "agonize." Paul and Timothy labor and suffer because they trust in the living God, "who is the Savior of all men, especially of those who believe."

The word "especially" is *malista* (μάλιστα)—chiefly, most of all, above all. God is the Savior of all men in the sense that Jesus's death on the cross made a way for every human being. First John 2:2 says He is the propitiation "not for ours only, but also for the whole world." Second Peter speaks of false teachers who "deny the Lord who bought them"—even they were purchased. A way has been made for all; every man, woman, and child has the opportunity to come to the Lord. But not all will believe. While God is the Savior of all in provision, He is "especially" the Savior of those who believe—they experience salvation's benefits: not just fire insurance, but power, protection, strength, courage, and peace.

Let No One Despise Your Youth

"Let no one despise your youth, but be an example to the believers in word, in conduct, in love, in spirit, in faith, in purity."
(1 Timothy 4:12)

The word "youth" is *neotēs* (νεότης), from which we get "neophyte." In ancient Greek usage, it typically referred to anyone under forty. Timothy was probably in his mid-thirties at this point. Youth is subjective: forty feels ancient if someone is still single and hoping to marry, but extremely young for a president or for a pastor leading a congregation with many older members.

Paul's instruction is that Timothy should not let anyone despise his youth. The solution? "Be an example to the believers." The grammar indicates an ongoing action—"keep on being an example." It was already happening; it needed to continue. Paul wrote in 1 Corinthians 11:1, "Imitate me, just as I also imitate Christ." Some forty-year-olds are less mature than certain teenagers. Some young people in their teens and twenties display remarkable maturity. One of my favorite pastors often says, "God is willing to make young men old in the days in which we

71

live"—He is looking for people who are willing, and if they want to be mature, He will pour out maturity upon them. No one is too old to start; no one is too young to be used. If someone feels they stagnated in faith for thirty years, starting now, God will accelerate their growth. Timothy was mature, and Paul urged him to keep being mature, to keep being an example. If believers walk out the spiritual life faithfully, age becomes irrelevant—people will respect them because they are watching.

Paul lists six areas for being an example. *In word*: what comes out of the mouth matters. A little gossip, a little slander, can wipe away a testimony built over years. *In conduct*: general behavior and lifestyle. *In love*: specific acts of sacrificial, *agape* love that others can observe. *In spirit*: this is lowercase "spirit"—disposition and attitude. Christians should not be perpetually gloomy. Sorrow and discouragement come, but they should not define the believer. With the living God, with eternity secured, with sins forgiven, with a mansion being prepared—there is much to be joyful about. Even in difficult seasons, gratitude helps; things could always be worse. *In faith*: the spiritual walk itself, something others can admire and be encouraged by. *In purity*: sanctification, freedom from sin. Seeing others walk successfully gives hope that one can walk successfully too.

Reading, Exhortation, and Doctrine

"Till I come, give attention to reading, to exhortation, to doctrine. Do not neglect the gift that is in you, which was given to you by prophecy with the laying on of the hands of the eldership. Meditate on these things; give yourself entirely to them, that your progress may be evident to all." (1 Timothy 4:13-15)

All three items—"the reading, the exhortation, the doctrine"—have definite articles in Greek. "The reading" is *anagnōsis* (ἀνάγνωσις), a word used for public reading, most often of Scripture. The ESV and NIV helpfully translate it "the public reading of Scripture." This was essential in a time when most people did not own personal copies of the Bible. "The exhortation" refers to encouragement and application. "The doctrine" refers to teaching—the content of the faith.

Paul then urges Timothy: "Do not neglect the gift that is in you." The word "gift" is *charisma* (χάρισμα)—the same word used for spiritual gifts throughout the New Testament. Romans 12:6 says believers have "gifts differing according to the grace given to us." First Corinthians 12 explains that "there are diversities of gifts, but the same Spirit... the manifestation of the Spirit is given to each one for the profit of all... one and the same Spirit works all these things, distributing to each one individually as He wills."

Believers do not choose their gifts; the Spirit distributes them. But gifts can be neglected. Ephesians 4:16 describes the body of Christ as "joined and knit together by what every joint supplies, according to the effective working by which every part does its share." What happens when body parts neglect their gifts? The whole body suffers. If all Christians are given spiritual gifts, how many are neglecting them? The Church would see major traction if every believer actively engaged daily in the ministry God designed them for.

Timothy's gift was given "by prophecy with the laying on of the hands of the eldership." Acts records that before Paul and Barnabas went on their first missionary journey, prophets among the believers spoke, and hands were laid on them to commission them. Perhaps when Paul picked up

Timothy at Lystra on his second missionary journey, elders there recognized Timothy's gifts through prophecy and laid hands on him, commissioning him for service. This is something every believer can seek: to know their gifts and be willing to use them.

"Meditate on these things; give yourself entirely to them, that your progress may be evident to all." This is not pride or arrogance. Jesus said no one lights a lamp and hides it under a basket; it is set on a stand so all can see. A city on a hill cannot be hidden. Believers should want their progress to be evident—not for self-glorification, but so that others "may see your good works and glorify your Father in heaven." Give yourself entirely to these things so that everyone, inside and outside The Church, can see the reality of a Spirit-filled life.

Take Heed to Yourself and to the Doctrine

> *"Take heed to yourself and to the doctrine.*
> *Continue in them, for in doing this you will*
> *save both yourself and those who hear you."*
> *(1 Timothy 4:16)*

Paul tells Timothy to take care of himself. In the next chapter, Paul will tell Timothy to take a little wine with his water because Timothy was having health issues. Many pastors neglect taking care of themselves, and it hurts in the long run—neglecting health, neglecting family.

David Brainerd and Robert Murray M'Cheyne both died at twenty-nine, essentially working themselves to death. Was that the Lord's will? Brainerd was a missionary to Native Americans whose journals, compiled by Jonathan Edwards, have inspired countless believers. Leonard Ravenhill and others looked to Brainerd as a powerhouse of prayer.

M'Cheyne saw revival in Scotland and created the
M'Cheyne Bible Reading Plan still used by many today.
E.M. Bounds quoted M'Cheyne extensively in *Power
Through Prayer*. These men accomplished much—but
perhaps, had they taken better care of themselves, they
would have produced twice as much.

In contrast, George Mueller, who had serious lung
problems requiring him to leave the city periodically for
better air, lived into his nineties because he took breaks
when needed. In Paul's day and in the nineteenth century,
disease and illness were rampant, and life expectancy was
low. Modern medicine has extended lifespans significantly.
But the enemy is cunning: for every physical illness
conquered, mental health challenges seem to have
increased. The information age overwhelms people,
bringing anxiety, fear, and oppression. Once, a person
worked hard in the fields, came home, and had no idea
what happened in town because no one went that day. Hard
work, good sleep, limited information. Today, information
floods in constantly—more than humans were designed to
process over six thousand years of history. This may
explain the prevalence of depression and anxiety.

So Paul's instruction applies to every believer: take heed to
yourself. Pay attention if a break is needed. Take care of
physical and mental health. And take heed to the doctrine—
The Church, the ministry. Do both. "Continue in them, for
in doing this you will save both yourself and those who
hear you." This is not salvation by works; it echoes
Philippians 2:12—"work out your own salvation with fear
and trembling." Taking heed results in experiencing all of
God's gifts, His peace, and the fullness of what salvation
provides.

Priorities

Christ must come first. Always. If that part is not right, everything else falls apart. Then spouse—before children, because children need parents with a strong marriage. Then children. Then ministry—and ministry does not mean only official church positions. Every believer was fearfully and wonderfully made to serve a purpose in the body of Christ, gifted by the Holy Spirit for that purpose. Then vocation. Then hobbies and everything else.

A word of clarification: just because something is lower on the priority list does not mean it demands less time. A wife is second on the list, but she appreciates having the power on and food in the refrigerator—so more waking hours may be spent at work than with her. The question is: where does the buck stop? What comes first when priorities conflict? If priorities are truly ordered correctly, decisions become clearer.

The danger is when stated priorities do not match actual priorities. Someone might claim God comes first, but when listing everything that receives time and attention—job, health, extended family, friends, hobbies, sports, rest, and then finally Bible reading and prayer near the bottom— something is wrong. If God truly comes first, daily Bible reading needs to be a high priority. If family matters, the budget needs attention. Prayer and church attendance need to be high priorities, not afterthoughts squeezed in after everything else.

Run to Win

The closing exhortation ties everything together with the athletic imagery Paul loves:

> *"Therefore we also, since we are surrounded by so great a cloud of witnesses, let us lay aside every weight, and the sin which so easily ensnares us, and let us run with endurance the race that is set before us." (Hebrews 12:1)*

> *"Do you not know that those who run in a race all run, but one receives the prize? Run in such a way that you may obtain it. And everyone who competes for the prize is temperate in all things. Now they do it to obtain a perishable crown, but we for an imperishable crown. Therefore I run thus: not with uncertainty. Thus I fight: not as one who beats the air. But I discipline my body and bring it into subjection, lest, when I have preached to others, I myself should become disqualified." (1 Corinthians 9:24-27)*

Paul had a calling: to preach to others. He did not want to become disqualified. Every believer has a calling too—one from which they could be disqualified by choosing to sit on the sidelines. But the exhortation is clear: meditate on these things, give yourself entirely to them, let progress be evident to all. Do not neglect the gifts God has given. Use them. Seek them. Bodily exercise has value, but godliness is profitable for all things—for this life and the one to come.

The Pastoral Epistles

These are the exhortations for holding fast in hard times. In the latter days, with false teaching abounding and the enemy prowling, believers must cling to sound doctrine, exercise toward godliness, take heed to themselves, and run the race to win.

Honoring Others and Guarding Hearts
1 Timothy 5-6

First Timothy 5 through 6:2 forms a cohesive unit focused on honoring different groups of people: older and younger men and women, widows, elders, and masters. The remainder of chapter 6 addresses error, greed, contentment, and the call to fight the good fight of faith. This is practical, straightforward instruction for how The Church ought to function and how believers ought to live.

Honoring Men and Women

> *"Do not rebuke an older man, but exhort him as a father, younger men as brothers, older women as mothers, younger women as sisters, with all purity." (1 Timothy 5:1-2)*

The word "older man" is *presbyteros* (πρεσβύτερος)—the same word translated "elder" when referring to church leadership. Like in English, the word has two meanings: an older man in general, and the official position of elder. Here Paul is speaking of older men generally, not the office of elder (which he will address later in the chapter).

The word "rebuke" here is unusual. It is not the typical New Testament word for rebuke (*elegchō*, meaning to correct or find fault). Instead, Paul uses *epiplēssō* (ἐπιπλήσσω), a strong word appearing only here in the New Testament. It literally combines *epi* (upon) and *plēssō* (to strike or hit)—essentially, "to beat up." Paul is not saying an older man cannot be corrected; he is saying do not beat him up. If correction is needed, it must be done tactfully and respectfully. Exhort him as a father.

Younger men, by contrast, can be addressed as brothers. There is a place for more direct correction among peers. With a brother, one can be a little more firm—always loving, always tactful, but more direct than with an elder. Older women should be treated as mothers, with the same respect given to one's own mother.

Younger women are to be treated as sisters, "with all purity." This is excellent advice for any man, but especially for a young pastor. What kind of thoughts does a man have about his sister? That is the boundary for thoughts about women in the body of Christ. What kind of advances does a man make toward his sister? None—and that is how all women should be treated until after a wedding ceremony and the exchange of vows. Prior to that, treat her like a sister with all purity. This establishes healthy boundaries and removes any grounds for blame or suspicion.

Honoring Widows

From verse 3 through verse 16, Paul addresses widows at length. In that time and culture, an older woman without a husband was often destitute—unable to find work, unable to provide for herself. The early church maintained a register of widows whom The Church would fully support. This practice had precedent in Israel's history.

Jephthah's daughter in Judges 11, by my interpretation, was not sacrificed but committed to service at the tabernacle—which is why they bewailed her virginity, for women who committed themselves to such service remained there for life. Judges 21 mentions women who lived at the tabernacle. First Samuel 2:22 records that Hophni and Phinehas, Eli's wicked sons, were sleeping with women who served at the tabernacle entrance. And in the New Testament, Anna the prophetess is a beautiful example: widowed after many years of marriage, she lived at the temple, serving and worshiping, praying and fasting (Luke 2:36-38). This was never commanded but was a provision for those who desired it.

> *"Honor widows who are really widows. But*
> *if any widow has children or grandchildren,*
> *let them first learn to show piety at home*
> *and to repay their parents; for this is good*
> *and acceptable before God."*
> *(1 Timothy 5:3-4)*

Paul immediately clarifies what constitutes a "real" widow deserving of church support. If a widow has children or grandchildren, they should care for her. The text says they should "repay" their parents—not pay, but *repay*, because parents poured into their children. This is basic piety before God.

> *"Now she who is really a widow, and left*
> *alone, trusts in God and continues in*
> *supplications and prayers night and day.*
> *But she who lives in pleasure is dead while*
> *she lives." (1 Timothy 5:5-6)*

A true widow—one who has no one—is characterized by trusting God, continuing in prayer, seeking the Lord for provision. If a woman claiming to be a widow is instead living in pleasure, she demonstrates that she is not a believing woman and is not among those The Church should support.

> *"But if anyone does not provide for his own,*
> *and especially for those of his household, he*
> *has denied the faith and is worse than an*
> *unbeliever." (1 Timothy 5:8)*

This is a strong statement. Even unbelievers understand that people should care for their parents. Jesus addressed this with the Pharisees, who used "Corban" (dedicated to God) as a loophole to avoid caring for parents. They would declare their resources dedicated to the Lord so they could not give to their mother or father. Jesus condemned this as nullifying God's command through human tradition. Paul says plainly: someone who does not provide for his own household has denied the faith and is worse than an unbeliever. "His own" likely refers to extended relatives— aunts, uncles, cousins, the broader church family. "Those of his household" refers to the inner circle: parents, siblings, children. Wife and children are not mentioned because it would be unthinkable for a man not to provide for them.

Requirements for Enrolled Widows

> *"Do not let a widow under sixty years old be taken into the number, and not unless she has been the wife of one man, well reported for good works: if she has brought up children, if she has lodged strangers, if she has washed the saints' feet, if she has relieved the afflicted, if she has diligently followed every good work."*
> *(1 Timothy 5:9-10)*

The minimum age of sixty must be understood in context. Life expectancy in the first-century Roman Empire averaged around twenty to thirty years when including infant mortality. Excluding infant and toddler deaths, one study placed the average lifespan at thirty-six for women and forty-two for men—with women's average lower because approximately thirty percent of women eventually died in childbirth. If a woman lived to her fifties, she was doing well. If she reached sixty, she was old by ancient standards. This limitation restricted church support to those who were truly elderly and destitute.

"The wife of one man" is the exact grammatical opposite of the requirement for overseers in chapter 3 ("husband of one wife"). As discussed there, this speaks of character—a faithful, devoted woman, not one who has been married repeatedly with multiple divorced husbands still living. The list of good works—bringing up children, lodging strangers, washing the saints' feet, relieving the afflicted— is not a checklist where every box must be marked but a description of a godly woman who has lived faithfully. Anna from Luke 2 exemplifies this kind of woman.

Younger Widows

> *"But refuse the younger widows; for when they have begun to grow wanton against Christ, they desire to marry, having condemnation because they have cast off their first faith. And besides they learn to be idle, wandering about from house to house, and not only idle but also gossips and busybodies, saying things which they ought not." (1 Timothy 5:11-13)*

The concept was that those enrolled under the church's provision were committing to a life of service—they were not expected to leave. Paul warns that younger widows should not make such a commitment. In time, a young woman may desire marriage and children. If she has committed to lifelong service, she faces a painful choice: break her commitment or suppress God-given desires. This actually serves as a strong argument against the practice of requiring young women to take permanent religious vows. Paul's solution is simple: do not put young women in this situation.

Furthermore, if young widows are given provision without responsibility, they may become idle, wandering from house to house, becoming gossips and busybodies. Gossip is not a minor sin. Romans 1:29 places "whisperers" (the ESV translates it "gossips") right alongside murderers in a list of wickedness. If someone wants to murder a church, gossip will do it. Whispering and talking create division. Sometimes gossip masquerades as "venting," but when bitterness drives someone to share grievances with others, many become defiled (Hebrews 12:15). One of the healthiest things believers can do is simply stop gossip when they hear it: "That sounds like gossip. I don't want to hear it." It may sting, but any believer with maturity will receive the correction.

> *"Therefore I desire that the younger widows marry, bear children, manage the house, give no opportunity to the adversary to speak reproachfully." (1 Timothy 5:14)*

The word "widows" is actually supplied by translators; the Greek simply says "younger women." Paul desires that younger women marry, bear children, and manage the house—giving no opportunity for the adversary to speak reproachfully. This is not a popular verse in modern culture, but it is godly. God calls it good for women to marry, bear children, and manage the home. This is not the *only* pursuit for women, nor is it the pursuit of *every* woman. But The Church must make clear that this is a good and godly pursuit with no shame attached.

Years ago, while teaching high school, I asked a group of senior girls how many expected to become stay-at-home mothers. Not one raised her hand. Yet I knew that life would lead many of them there. Because none were steering in that direction, they would likely spend time and money on paths they would eventually leave. The adversary works to lure women away from God's design. Satan attacks anything God designed: marriage, gender roles, sexuality, parenting. Here Paul warns that some have already "turned aside after Satan" (verse 15).

Verse 16 summarizes: if any believing man or woman has widows in their family, let them provide for them so The Church is not burdened—freeing resources for those who are truly destitute. The Church must be discerning about benevolence, not giving whimsically but ensuring resources remain available for those with genuine need.

Honoring Elders

"Let the elders who rule well be counted worthy of double honor, especially those who labor in the word and doctrine. For the Scripture says, 'You shall not muzzle an ox while it treads out the grain,' and, 'The laborer is worthy of his wages.'"
(1 Timothy 5:17-18)

Now Paul shifts to church elders—the official leadership. There has been long-standing debate about what "double honor" means. Some have complicated interpretations, but the simplest reading is this: elders who rule well deserve good compensation. Those doing the work are worthy of being paid, and those doing it exceptionally well are worthy of being paid well. This applies especially to those who labor in the word and doctrine—the pastor-teacher who oversees the main teaching ministry.

Paul quotes two passages: Deuteronomy 25:4 ("You shall not muzzle an ox while it treads out the grain") and Luke 10:7 ("The laborer is worthy of his wages"). Notice what Paul writes: "the *Scripture* says"—and grammatically, the conjunction ties both quotations together as Scripture. This is remarkable: Paul the apostle, writing around AD 63-64, is recognizing Luke's Gospel as Scripture. That term was not used lightly; it referred to the inspired Word of God. This also helps date Luke's Gospel as written before this letter. Paul makes the same argument about paying pastors in 1 Corinthians 9 using the Deuteronomy passage. It is right and good to compensate those who labor in ministry.

Accusations Against Elders

> *"Do not receive an accusation against an*
> *elder except from two or three witnesses.*
> *Those who are sinning rebuke in the*
> *presence of all, that the rest also may fear."*
> *(1 Timothy 5:19-20)*

The two-or-three-witness requirement appears throughout Scripture. Jesus invokes it in Matthew 18 for church discipline. Deuteronomy 19:15-21 establishes the principle: one witness cannot bring a charge; the matter must be established by multiple witnesses. Furthermore, if a witness is found to be false, he receives the penalty he sought to impose on the accused. This was meant to discourage frivolous or malicious accusations.

As Homer Kent observed: "This safeguard of the elder is a wise one. No person is more subject to Satan's attack in the form of gossip and slander than God's servant. If every accusation necessitated a full investigation, the elder would have time for little else. Therefore, no elder should be brought to trial on the accusation of one person, for even charges of which an elder is acquitted can damage his work."

When one person brings an accusation that seems out of character for the accused, wisdom suggests taking it with a grain of salt. Perhaps the accuser was angry and retold the story differently than it happened. But when multiple witnesses confirm wrongdoing, the matter is serious.

This is a two-edged sword. If an elder is found guilty, verse 20 says to "rebuke in the presence of all, that the rest also may fear." When ordinary members sin, Proverbs 10:12 applies: "Love covers all sins." Proverbs 17:9 adds: "He who covers a transgression seeks love, but he who repeats a matter separates friends." Not every sin requires public exposure. But when leaders fall, it affects the whole church. The healthiest approach is often to address it publicly—not with salacious details, but with enough information to answer questions so the matter can be closed. Otherwise, unanswered questions breed gossip: "Did you hear what happened? What do you know?" Speaking plainly prevents a gossip storm.

The principle extends beyond church leadership: public sin deserves public confession. Not every sin requires public acknowledgment, but when sin is committed publicly— when everyone sees it—the confession should match. Someone who says something foolish online should publicly, on the same platform, repent and ask forgiveness. Someone who behaves wrongly at work should acknowledge it to those who witnessed it. The unbelieving world is accustomed to seeing Christians sin; they are not accustomed to seeing Christians confess. But they should.

Ordaining Elders Carefully

"I charge you before God and the Lord Jesus Christ and the elect angels that you observe these things without prejudice, doing nothing with partiality. Do not lay hands on anyone hastily, nor share in other

people's sins; keep yourself pure."
(1 Timothy 5:21-22)

Paul charges Timothy solemnly—before God, before Christ, before the elect angels—to handle these matters seriously. "Laying on of hands" refers to ordaining or commissioning elders. Paul warns: do not ordain anyone hastily. Take time to verify that candidates are who they claim to be. If Timothy's haste places someone in a position of power and influence who then harms people, Timothy shares in those sins.

> *"Some men's sins are clearly evident,*
> *preceding them to judgment, but those of*
> *some men follow later. Likewise, the good*
> *works of some are clearly evident, and those*
> *that are otherwise cannot be hidden."*
> *(1 Timothy 5:24-25)*

Some people's sins are obvious—everyone can see them. But some have hidden sins that only emerge later despite due diligence. Paul encourages Timothy: do your best, but do not stress over what you cannot know. Luke 8:17 reminds us that nothing secret will remain hidden forever. Likewise, good works—even secret ones—will eventually be revealed, certainly at the judgment seat of Christ. The point is to exercise care without being paralyzed by fear of the unknown.

A Word About Wine

> *"No longer drink only water, but use a little*
> *wine for your stomach's sake and your*
> *frequent infirmities." (1 Timothy 5:23)*

This verse appears almost as an aside. Paul tells Timothy to keep himself pure, and then seems to remember: "But not *too* pure, Timothy." The phrase "no longer drink only water" indicates that Timothy had been drinking only water—he completely abstained from alcohol. He took the instruction that a bishop should "not be given to wine" very seriously.

But Timothy had stomach problems and frequent infirmities. Paul advises him to add a little wine to his water. In the ancient world, water often went bad. It would develop contaminants over time. Sailing ships crossing the Atlantic carried more beer than water because water spoiled midway through the voyage while alcohol preserved. Adding wine to water helped purify it. Additionally, ancient wine was significantly weaker than modern alcoholic beverages—approximately one-sixth to one-eighth the strength of a modern glass of wine due to fermentation methods and the practice of diluting with water. This is important for those who note that "Jesus drank wine" when defending their drinking habits because to reach the equivalent effect of one glass of modern wine, a person from Bible times would need to drink six to eight glasses of ancient wine.

Paul is not endorsing drunkenness but addressing a health issue. Timothy had a conviction about purity, but Paul reminds him not to let that conviction reach an illogical level that harms his body. This is medicinal advice. It also counters the teaching of some religious groups that reject all medicine and doctors as lacking faith. Paul the apostle is telling Timothy to take medicine.

Honoring Masters

"Let as many bondservants as are under the yoke count their own masters worthy of all honor, so that the name of God and His doctrine may not be blasphemed. And those

89

> *who have believing masters, let them not*
> *despise them because they are brethren, but*
> *rather serve them because those who are*
> *benefited are believers and beloved."*
> *(1 Timothy 6:1-2)*

Verse 1 addresses unbelieving masters, while verse 2 specifies believing masters. For those with unbelieving employers, work performance is a testimony. Unbelievers may never read the Gospels, but they observe how Christians work, behave, speak, and demonstrate ethics. Work hard, Paul says, so that God's name and doctrine are not blasphemed.

For those with believing masters, the temptation might be to expect preferential treatment: "We're brothers—why don't you make me part owner? Why don't I get a promotion?" Paul says not to despise believing masters because of unmet expectations. A Christian employer is not obligated to break business agreements or give free services simply because an employee shares the faith. A Christian plumber cannot do every believer's plumbing for free—he has bills to pay. A Christian landlord cannot give free rent—she has expenses too. Believers should always be generous and loving, but business relationships have legitimate boundaries. Brotherhood does not nullify financial realities.

Error and Greed

> *"If anyone teaches otherwise and does not*
> *consent to wholesome words, even the words*
> *of our Lord Jesus Christ, and to the doctrine*
> *which accords with godliness, he is proud,*
> *knowing nothing, but is obsessed with*
> *disputes and arguments over words, from*
> *which come envy, strife, reviling, evil*

suspicions, useless wranglings of men of
corrupt minds and destitute of the truth, who
suppose that godliness is a means of gain.
From such withdraw yourself."
(1 Timothy 6:3-5)

Paul describes people who think Christianity is a path to earthly gain—power, prominence, money through ministry. But even beyond financial motives, he describes those who do not stick to sound doctrine, who are proud and obsessed with disputes. From such people, withdraw. Once it becomes clear that someone has no interest in logic, reason, or truth—that they are simply fishing for arguments—disengage.

I encountered this in an online discussion. Someone posed what seemed like a sincere question about when the Bible permitted eating meat. I pointed to Genesis 9, after the flood. He raised another objection. I cited 1 Timothy 4, which identifies forbidding foods as a false teaching. He kept going until he argued that "the narrow way" means eating only vegetables. At that point, it was clear this was useless wrangling. Some people—perhaps even family members or old friends of yours—are simply looking for disputes. It does not mean abandoning the relationship, but when conversations steer toward fruitless arguments, drop it and move on. If their heart softens, the opportunity for genuine discussion may return.

Godliness with Contentment

"Now godliness with contentment is great
gain. For we brought nothing into this
world, and it is certain we can carry nothing
out. And having food and clothing, with
these we shall be content."
(1 Timothy 6:6-8)

91

The contrast is beautiful. Those false teachers supposed godliness was a means to earthly gain. But true godliness *with contentment* is great gain—real gain. Learning contentment is one of the great struggles of life. Job understood: "Naked I came from my mother's womb, and naked shall I return there. The Lord gave, and the Lord has taken away; blessed be the name of the Lord" (Job 1:21). We brought nothing into this world; we carry nothing out. If we have food and clothing, we can be content.

The sin of covetousness deserves attention. The first nine commandments seem clear: do not murder, do not commit adultery, do not lie. But "do not covet"—what is so bad about wanting things? Covetousness is the thief of all joy. It causes people to despise what they have because they want what others have. Ecclesiastes 5:10 says, "He who loves silver will not be satisfied with silver." Wanting leads to needing more money, which leads to working more, which leaves no time for church, no time for devotions—all rooted in dissatisfaction with what God has provided.

Social media intensifies this struggle. We are constantly bombarded with images of what we do not have—other people's bodies, cars, vacations, meals. A hundred years ago, people worked farms and saw few others. They were not exposed to endless images of people who seemed to have more. Today, we see people at their prime and assume it is normal. We see romance in movies and think that is what marriage looks like, when real marriage involves conflict, growth, and iron sharpening iron. Covetousness sparks all manner of other sins because dissatisfaction drives people to seek fulfillment in wrong places.

I am a fitness enthusiast and confessed to my assisting pastor that when watching fitness videos online, the thought arises: "I wish I looked like him." Then comes the mental correction: "I'm in good shape. Better than most men my age. I should be thankful for where I am." We see images and think they are normal—but often they are not. Satan tries to define unrealistic standards as normal so that we feel inadequate with what God has given. The antidote is contentment. Philippians 4:11-13 says: "I have learned in whatever state I am, to be content: I know how to be abased, and I know how to abound... I can do all things through Christ who strengthens me." That famous verse is not about athletic achievements—it is about handling every situation, whether abundance or need, through Christ.

The Love of Money

> *"But those who desire to be rich fall into temptation and a snare, and into many foolish and harmful lusts which drown men in destruction and perdition. For the love of money is a root of all kinds of evil, for which some have strayed from the faith in their greediness, and pierced themselves through with many sorrows." (1 Timothy 6:9-10)*

"Those who desire" is present tense—those who are *continually* consumed with becoming rich. Such people fall into temptation, snares, foolish lusts, and ultimately destruction. Jesus warned in Matthew 13:22 about seed sown among thorns: the cares of this world and the deceitfulness of riches choke the word, making it unfruitful. Whether consumed by anxiety over daily needs or by chasing riches, both conditions represent eyes fixed on worldly things rather than seeking first His kingdom.

Verse 10 is often misquoted. Looking at the literal Greek word order it says: "A root for all the evils is the love of money." In Greek, if the definite article ("the") is absent, as it is in this verse, it indicates "a root" rather than "the root." Paul is not saying that all evil traces back to money as *the*

93

root. He is saying the love of money is *a* root that leads to every kind of evil. Which of the Ten Commandments has not been broken for financial gain? People compromise sexually for money. People murder for money. People lie, steal, and dishonor parents for money. The love of money is a root that branches into every category of sin.

But You, O Man of God

> *"But you, O man of God, flee these things and pursue righteousness, godliness, faith, love, patience, gentleness. Fight the good fight of faith, lay hold on eternal life, to which you were also called and have confessed the good confession in the presence of many witnesses."*
> *(1 Timothy 6:11-12)*

"Man of God"—in the Old Testament, this title belonged to Moses, Joshua, David, Elijah, Elisha, and the prophets. For Timothy, a young Jewish man, to hear Paul call him "man of God" must have been profound. This is not a title given lightly. Every believer can aspire to it. Second Timothy 3:16-17 explains how: "All Scripture is given by inspiration of God, and is profitable for doctrine, for reproof, for correction, for instruction in righteousness, that the man of God may be complete, thoroughly equipped for every good work." Keep digging into Scripture to be a man or woman of God.

Verses 11-12 contain three present active imperatives—commands to keep doing something continuously. *Keep on fleeing* these things: the love of money, useless disputes, all the destructive patterns Paul has described. One commentator wrote: "There is no safe distance. Just keep fleeing." Whatever sins especially trip you up, face the other direction and keep going. Head toward God, and you will be fleeing all sin. First Corinthians 6:18: "Flee sexual immorality." First Corinthians 10:14: "Flee from idolatry." Second Timothy 2:22: "Flee also youthful lusts." James 4:7 offers the flip side: "Submit to God. Resist the devil and he will flee from you." Not rebuke the devil, not cast him out—simply resist, and he flees.

Keep on pursuing righteousness, godliness, faith, love, patience, gentleness—essentially, the fruit of the Spirit. Keep pursuing even in areas of strength, because there are always areas of weakness. All these fruit are promised to every Spirit-filled believer. And pursue them alongside other believers; it need not be done alone.

Keep on fighting the good fight of faith. The word "fight" is *agōnizomai* (ἀγωνίζομαι)—the root of "agonize." Greek scholar Kenneth Wuest noted that in some Greek games, losers had their eyes gouged out. This is not a casual competition. Everything is on the line. Paul wrote in 1 Corinthians 9:24-27: "Do you not know that those who run in a race all run, but one receives the prize? Run in such a way that you may obtain it. And everyone who competes for the prize is temperate in all things... I discipline my body and bring it into subjection, lest, when I have preached to others, I myself should become disqualified."

The word "temperate" (*egkrateuomai*) appears only twice in the New Testament: here and in 1 Corinthians 7:9, where Paul says those who cannot exercise self-control should marry rather than burn with lust. Temperance means controlling even strong urges—for food, for comfort, for pleasure. Paul realized he could become disqualified. Any believer could. The call is to fight hard, not coast.

"Lay hold on eternal life" uses the aorist tense—a once-for-all action. This is not about earning salvation but about embracing one's calling, experiencing the fullness of salvation now, and living out the purpose for which God made each person.

The Final Charge

> *"I urge you in the sight of God who gives life to all things, and before Christ Jesus who witnessed the good confession before Pontius Pilate, that you keep this commandment without spot, blameless until our Lord Jesus Christ's appearing, which He will manifest in His own time—He who is the blessed and only Potentate, the King of kings and Lord of lords, who alone has immortality, dwelling in unapproachable light, whom no man has seen or can see, to whom be honor and everlasting power. Amen." (1 Timothy 6:13-16)*

Paul urges Timothy to keep fighting hard until Christ's appearing—which the Father will manifest in His own time, for only the Father knows the day and hour. This doxology celebrates God as the blessed and only Potentate, King of kings, Lord of lords, who alone has immortality, dwelling in unapproachable light. This seems almost like a closing, but Paul has three more verses.

Instructions to the Rich

> *"Command those who are rich in this present age not to be haughty, nor to trust in uncertain riches but in the living God, who gives us richly all things to enjoy. Let them do good, that they be rich in good works, ready to give, willing to share, storing up for themselves a good foundation for the time to*

come, that they may lay hold on eternal
life." (1 Timothy 6:17-19)

Being rich is not sinful. Otherwise, God made Abraham, Isaac, Jacob, David, and Solomon sinners by blessing them with wealth. The problem is desiring and chasing riches, or trusting in them rather than in God. Those who are rich should not be haughty or trust in uncertain earthly riches but in the living God who gives richly all things to enjoy. If God has blessed someone, they should enjoy it and be thankful.

The rich are commanded to do good, be rich in good works, ready to give, willing to share. By doing so, they store up "a good foundation for the time to come" and "lay hold on eternal life"—the same phrase from verse 12. This is not earning salvation; nothing in this passage suggests that. It means embracing why God made them. If God made someone wealthy, He did so for a reason: that they would be generous, ready to give, willing to share.

I had coffee recently with a wealthy believer—a ridiculously humble man. He mentioned that his financial advisor had asked for a forecast for the coming year. He said he could not provide one. When asked why, he explained: "God gives me everything I have. I have no idea what He will give next year. I just know He will always provide and I will always have what I need." He was generous beyond measure. His ministry was giving, and God blessed him for it. He did not win the lottery or inherit money; he worked hard, used the gifts God gave him, and saw fruit. Now he uses that blessing to bless others.

The principle applies to every gift. If God gave the gift of singing, practice and bless The Church. If God gave the gift of teaching, study and prepare. If God gave the gift of hospitality, cook and welcome people. Whatever the gift, embrace it, develop it, and use it. That is laying hold on eternal life—grabbing hold of why God made you and doing something about it. It will not fall into anyone's lap; gifts must be cultivated and deployed.

Guard What Was Committed

> *"O Timothy! Guard what was committed to your trust, avoiding the profane and idle babblings and contradictions of what is falsely called knowledge—by professing it some have strayed concerning the faith. Grace be with you. Amen."*
> *(1 Timothy 6:20-21)*

This is the shortest closing of any Pauline letter. Timothy is to guard what was committed to him, avoiding profane babblings and false knowledge. Some have strayed from the faith by embracing such things.

Reading this brings to mind a friend who was a mentor in my early days as a Christian—someone who strayed concerning the faith, becoming caught up in idle babblings and contradictions falsely called knowledge. I have a note in my Bible at this verse to pray for him whenever I see it. Pray for those who have wandered. Many are being deceived in these days. The Church must respond: love them, stay engaged, be proactive. Use whatever gifts God has given. If gifted in hospitality, do not wait for people to come—go to them. If gifted in counseling, do not wait for someone to ask for help—reach out. Start young with the next generation; do not wait until they are teenagers and far off. Pass on wisdom however God has gifted you.

The body of Christ must be in full working order in these days. People are being deceived, stolen from The Church by the enemy. Even if they are saved, they miss out on every blessing that comes from walking in obedience. So fight the good fight of faith. Keep going hard. Guard what was committed to you. Remember that some have strayed. Grace be with you. Amen.

The Pastoral Epistles

Sound Doctrine and Godly Living
Titus 1-3

Introduction to Titus

This is a short book. It follows a lot of what was covered in First Timothy. Titus and Timothy were both young pastors, both sons in the faith to Paul, and they followed Paul through many of his journeys. Both Titus and First Timothy were written right around the same time.

The reason we are going in the order of First Timothy, Titus, and then Second Timothy is because that is likely the order they were written. Some scholars say Titus may have come before First Timothy, but evidence suggests it probably came soon after. Both were written after Paul got out of prison.

After Paul was released from prison, he made a sweep through Asia Minor. He traveled by sea and left Titus on the island of Crete. He left Timothy in Ephesus. After moving on, he wrote First Timothy and Titus. Then he went off to Spain and back, did all that traveling, got imprisoned again, and from prison wrote Second Timothy during his second imprisonment.

Who Was Titus?

Titus is not mentioned a lot in the Bible. What is fascinating is that he is only mentioned in Galatians, Second Corinthians, and one verse in Second Timothy about sending him to Dalmatia. And of course, he has a book written to him. But he is not mentioned in the Book of Acts at all. He is one of those guys who does not get mentioned but is there behind the scenes throughout.

In Galatians 2, Paul says:

> *"Then after fourteen years I went up again to Jerusalem with Barnabas, and also took Titus with me. I went up by revelation, and communicated to them that gospel which I preach among the Gentiles, but privately to those who were of reputation, lest by any means I might run, or had run, in vain. Yet not even Titus who was with me, being a Greek, was compelled to be circumcised."*
> *(Galatians 2:1–3)*

There has been debate about what Paul is referring to here in Galatians—whether it was the trip for the Jerusalem Council or, as I believe, the earlier trip in Acts 11. Acts 11 is before the first missionary journey. Gentiles start getting saved in Antioch. That is where believers were first called Christians. Barnabas goes to Tarsus, which is not far from Antioch, picks up Paul, and brings him back.

At the very end of Acts 11, after Agabus prophesies about the famine in Jerusalem, Paul and Barnabas go up by revelation to tell the people in Jerusalem what is going on. They go up and privately talk about all the Gentiles who have been getting saved. And they brought one with them—his name was Titus. They did not want this guy to get circumcised because he was totally a Gentile, a Greek, not Jewish at all.

Timothy, who was half Jewish, got circumcised because they thought it would be a stumbling block for a Jewish person to see someone with Jewish heritage not following

Jewish custom. Timothy did it to accommodate Jewish believers. But not Titus.

We know Titus was with Paul on his third missionary journey because he is mentioned eight times in Second Corinthians. If you remember our study of Second Corinthians, there was a severe letter written to the Corinthians between First and Second Corinthians. Titus was the one who carried that letter. He came back, met Paul, and told Paul that it was received well—Paul had been harsh, and they took it. Paul writes Second Corinthians as a more gentle follow-up, and Titus takes that back as well.

We do not know for sure, but it seems they sent Titus because the Corinthians knew him well. If they knew Titus, he must have gone with Paul during his first or second missionary journey. Some scholars think Titus was with Paul the whole time—from Acts 11 all the way to the end, except for the times he carried those letters to Corinth. There are little hints that Titus was just always there. He was a young guy, probably similar in age to Timothy, helping out behind the scenes.

When Paul drops him off in Crete at the beginning of this book, it mentions that Titus had to have been with Paul as Paul was leaving his imprisonment. Did he go on the boat and get shipwrecked with Paul, or did he show up later? We do not know.

At the end of Second Timothy, Titus gets sent to Dalmatia—that is in the area of Croatia, up between Greece and Italy toward the top. Tradition holds that he eventually returned to Crete and died there.

The book is going to flow pretty easily because a lot of it is similar to First Timothy.

The Greeting

> *"Paul, a bondservant of God and an apostle
> of Jesus Christ, according to the faith of
> God's elect and the acknowledgment of the
> truth which accords with godliness, in hope
> of eternal life which God, who cannot lie,
> promised before time began, but has in due
> time manifested His word through
> preaching, which was committed to me
> according to the commandment of God our
> Savior—To Titus, a true son in our common
> faith: Grace, mercy, and peace from God
> the Father and the Lord Jesus Christ our
> Savior." (Titus 1:1–4)*

This introduction is like a normal Pauline introduction, but there is some extra content. Paul is connecting with another preacher, talking about things that would resonate with a fellow minister.

I want to point out something for later: in Titus 2:13, the phrase "our great God and Savior Jesus Christ" became a very commonly used title for Jesus in the early church by The Church fathers. Here in the greeting, we see "God our Savior" and "Jesus Christ our Savior," and then later "our great God and Savior Jesus Christ." Paul is nailing down the deity of Christ pretty clearly. For people who struggle to see the deity of Christ, you could throw out the whole Gospel of John where John hammers it home again and again—but even just here in Titus, Paul makes it unmistakable.

Titus's Assignment in Crete

> *"For this reason I left you in Crete, that you
> should set in order the things that are*

*lacking, and appoint elders in every city as I
commanded you." (Titus 1:5)*

Titus has an interesting role. He is somewhat like a bishop
in the sense that he is overseeing multiple churches on the
island and appointing elders in each city. His job is to set in
order the things that are lacking.

Paul then gives qualifications for elders that are very
similar to what we saw in First Timothy 3.

*"If a man is blameless, the husband of one
wife, having faithful children not accused of
dissipation or insubordination. For a bishop
must be blameless, as a steward of God, not
self-willed, not quick-tempered, not given to
wine, not violent, not greedy for money, but
hospitable, a lover of what is good,
sober-minded, just, holy, self-controlled,
holding fast the faithful word as he has been
taught, that he may be able, by sound
doctrine, both to exhort and convict those
who contradict." (Titus 1:6–9)*

We covered most of this in First Timothy, so I will not
belabor every point. But notice Paul uses "elder" and
"bishop" (or "overseer") interchangeably here. An elder
must be blameless—the husband of one wife, having
faithful children. A bishop must be blameless as a steward
of God. These are the same position described with two
different terms.

The qualifications are largely about character: not
self-willed, not quick-tempered, not given to wine, not
violent, not greedy for money. Positively: hospitable, a
lover of what is good, sober-minded, just, holy,
self-controlled. And then the functional requirement:
holding fast the faithful word as he has been taught, so that

105

he can exhort with sound doctrine and convict those who contradict.

This last point is crucial. Elders must be able to teach sound doctrine and refute false teaching. That is part of the job description.

The Problem of False Teachers

> *"For there are many insubordinate, both idle talkers and deceivers, especially those of the circumcision, whose mouths must be stopped, who subvert whole households, teaching things which they ought not, for the sake of dishonest gain." (Titus 1:10–11)*

Here is the problem Titus is facing: there are many insubordinate people, idle talkers and deceivers. Paul specifically mentions "those of the circumcision"—the Judaizers. These are people trying to put Gentile Christians under the Mosaic Law. Their mouths must be stopped because they are subverting whole households, teaching things they should not for the sake of dishonest gain.

This is why elders need to be able to convict those who contradict. False teachers were a serious problem in Crete.

> *"One of them, a prophet of their own, said, 'Cretans are always liars, evil beasts, lazy gluttons.' This testimony is true."*
> *(Titus 1:12–13a)*

Paul quotes Epimenides, a Cretan philosopher and poet from around 600 BC, who was considered a prophet by the Cretans themselves. The Cretans had a reputation even among themselves for being liars. In fact, to "Cretize" became a Greek word meaning to lie. Paul says this testimony is true—the reputation was earned.

"Therefore rebuke them sharply, that they
may be sound in the faith, not giving heed to
Jewish fables and commandments of men
who turn from the truth." (Titus 1:13b–14)

Titus is to rebuke them sharply so they may be sound in the faith. They are not to give heed to Jewish fables and commandments of men who turn from the truth. This parallels what Paul wrote to Timothy about myths and endless genealogies.

"To the pure all things are pure, but to those
who are defiled and unbelieving nothing is
pure; but even their mind and conscience
are defiled. They profess to know God, but
in works they deny Him, being abominable,
disobedient, and disqualified for every good
work." (Titus 1:15–16)

To the pure, all things are pure. But to those who are defiled and unbelieving, nothing is pure—their mind and conscience are defiled. They profess to know God, but their works deny Him. They are disqualified for every good work.

This is a sobering assessment. There are people who claim to know God but whose lives completely contradict that claim. Their profession is empty.

Sound Doctrine and Godly Living

Chapter 2 shifts from dealing with false teachers to positive instruction about what sound doctrine looks like in practice.

"But as for you, speak the things which are
proper for sound doctrine." (Titus 2:1)

Sound doctrine is not just about correct beliefs in the abstract. Sound doctrine produces godly living. Paul is going to show what that looks like for different groups in The Church.

Older Men

> *"That the older men be sober, reverent, temperate, sound in faith, in love, in patience." (Titus 2:2)*

Older men are to be sober, reverent, temperate, sound in faith, love, and patience. These are the character qualities that should mark a mature Christian man.

Older Women

> *"The older women likewise, that they be reverent in behavior, not slanderers, not given to much wine, teachers of good things—that they admonish the young women to love their husbands, to love their children, to be discreet, chaste, homemakers, good, obedient to their own husbands, that the word of God may not be blasphemed." (Titus 2:3–5)*

Older women are to be reverent in behavior, not slanderers, not given to much wine, teachers of good things. And what are they to teach? They are to admonish the younger women.

Notice what the younger women are to be taught: to love their husbands, to love their children, to be discreet, chaste, homemakers, good, obedient to their own husbands. The purpose is "that the word of God may not be blasphemed."

How we live either adorns the gospel or brings reproach upon it.

This is similar to what we saw in First Timothy 5:14 about younger women marrying, bearing children, and managing the house. It is a good and godly pursuit. The older women are to be the ones teaching and modeling this for the younger women.

Younger Men

> *"Likewise, exhort the young men to be sober-minded, in all things showing yourself to be a pattern of good works; in doctrine showing integrity, reverence, incorruptibility, sound speech that cannot be condemned, that one who is an opponent may be ashamed, having nothing evil to say of you." (Titus 2:6–8)*

Young men are to be sober-minded. Titus himself, as a young man, is to be a pattern of good works—showing integrity, reverence, incorruptibility, and sound speech that cannot be condemned. The goal is that opponents will have nothing evil to say.

Bondservants

> *"Exhort bondservants to be obedient to their own masters, to be well pleasing in all things, not answering back, not pilfering, but showing all good fidelity, that they may adorn the doctrine of God our Savior in all things." (Titus 2:9–10)*

Bondservants—or in our context, employees—are to be obedient to their masters, well pleasing, not answering back, not stealing, but showing all good fidelity. Why? "That they may adorn the doctrine of God our Savior in all things."

There is that phrase again: "God our Savior." And notice the purpose: our conduct adorns the doctrine. The way we live makes the gospel attractive or unattractive to the watching world.

The Grace of God

Now Paul gives the theological foundation for all this godly living:

> *"For the grace of God that brings salvation
> has appeared to all men, teaching us that,
> denying ungodliness and worldly lusts, we
> should live soberly, righteously, and godly
> in the present age, looking for the blessed
> hope and glorious appearing of our great
> God and Savior Jesus Christ, who gave
> Himself for us, that He might redeem us
> from every lawless deed and purify for
> Himself His own special people, zealous for
> good works." (Titus 2:11–14)*

This is one of the great passages on grace in the New Testament. The grace of God that brings salvation has appeared to all men. It is available to everyone.

And what does grace teach us? Grace teaches us to deny ungodliness and worldly lusts, and to live soberly, righteously, and godly in the present age. Grace is not a license to sin—grace teaches us to live holy lives.

We are looking for "the blessed hope and glorious appearing of our great God and Savior Jesus Christ." There is that phrase from the early church fathers: our great God and Savior Jesus Christ. His deity is unmistakable.

Why did He give Himself for us? "That He might redeem us from every lawless deed and purify for Himself His own special people, zealous for good works."

Grace produces zeal for good works. This is the consistent teaching of the New Testament. We are not saved by works, but we are saved for works. Ephesians 2:8–10 says we are saved by grace through faith, not of works—but we are created in Christ Jesus for good works, which God prepared beforehand that we should walk in them.

> *"Speak these things, exhort, and rebuke with*
> *all authority. Let no one despise you."*
> *(Titus 2:15)*

Titus is to speak these things, exhort, and rebuke with all authority. He is not to let anyone despise him. This echoes what Paul told Timothy: "Let no one despise your youth."

Good Works and Good Citizenship

> *"Remind them to be subject to rulers and*
> *authorities, to obey, to be ready for every*
> *good work, to speak evil of no one, to be*
> *peaceable, gentle, showing all humility to all*
> *men." (Titus 3:1–2)*

Paul tells Titus to remind the believers to be subject to rulers and authorities, to obey, to be ready for every good work. They are to speak evil of no one, to be peaceable, gentle, showing all humility to all men.

Christians are to be good citizens and good neighbors. We are not to be known for speaking evil of people or being contentious. We are to be known for gentleness and humility.

Our Former Condition

> *"For we ourselves were also once foolish, disobedient, deceived, serving various lusts and pleasures, living in malice and envy, hateful and hating one another." (Titus 3:3)*

Paul reminds Titus—and us—of what we used to be. We were foolish, disobedient, deceived, serving various lusts and pleasures, living in malice and envy, hateful and hating one another. That is what we were apart from Christ.

The Kindness and Love of God

> *"But when the kindness and the love of God our Savior toward man appeared, not by works of righteousness which we have done, but according to His mercy He saved us, through the washing of regeneration and renewing of the Holy Spirit, whom He poured out on us abundantly through Jesus Christ our Savior, that having been justified by His grace we should become heirs according to the hope of eternal life."*
> *(Titus 3:4–7)*

Here is the gospel in a nutshell. When the kindness and love of God our Savior appeared, He saved us—not by works of righteousness which we have done, but according to His mercy. It is all of grace.

He saved us through the washing of regeneration and renewing of the Holy Spirit. The Spirit has been poured out on us abundantly through Jesus Christ our Savior. Having been justified by His grace, we have become heirs according to the hope of eternal life.

Notice again: "God our Savior" and "Jesus Christ our Savior." The deity of Christ runs throughout this letter.

A Faithful Saying

> *"This is a faithful saying, and these things I want you to affirm constantly, that those who have believed in God should be careful to maintain good works. These things are good and profitable for men." (Titus 3:8)*

There is that phrase again: "This is a faithful saying." We saw it multiple times in First Timothy. Paul wants Titus to affirm constantly that those who have believed in God should be careful to maintain good works. These things are good and profitable for men.

Belief and behavior go together. Those who have believed should be careful to maintain good works. Not to earn salvation, but because that is what saved people do. That is the fruit of genuine faith.

Avoiding Foolish Disputes

> *"But avoid foolish disputes, genealogies, contentions, and strivings about the law; for they are unprofitable and useless."*
> *(Titus 3:9)*

This echoes what Paul wrote to Timothy about myths, endless genealogies, and disputes. These things are unprofitable and useless. Do not waste time on them.

> *"Reject a divisive man after the first and second admonition, knowing that such a*

person is warped and sinning, being
self-condemned." (Titus 3:10–11)

A divisive man—a factious person—is to be rejected after
the first and second admonition. Such a person is warped
and sinning, being self-condemned. The Church cannot
tolerate those who constantly stir up division. After proper
warning, they are to be rejected.

This is not about rejecting people who have honest
questions or disagreements. This is about people who are
factious, who love to divide, who thrive on controversy.
After two warnings, you are done with them.

Final Instructions and Greetings

"When I send Artemas to you, or Tychicus,
be diligent to come to me at Nicopolis, for I
have decided to spend the winter there. Send
Zenas the lawyer and Apollos on their
journey with haste, that they may lack
nothing. And let our people also learn to
maintain good works, to meet urgent needs,
that they may not be unfruitful." (Titus 3:12–
14)

Paul gives some personal instructions. He is going to send
Artemas or Tychicus to relieve Titus, and then Titus should
come to Paul at Nicopolis where he plans to spend the
winter. Titus is to send Zenas the lawyer and Apollos on
their journey with haste, making sure they lack nothing.

And then he repeats the theme one more time: let our
people learn to maintain good works, to meet urgent needs,
that they may not be unfruitful. Good works. Fruitfulness.
That is the mark of a healthy Christian and a healthy
church.

114

"All who are with me greet you. Greet those who love us in the faith. Grace be with you all. Amen." (Titus 3:15)

That is a warm closing. Grace be with you all.

In Closing

The theme that runs throughout this book is the connection between sound doctrine and godly living. What we believe shapes how we live. Grace teaches us to deny ungodliness. Faith produces works. Those who have believed should be careful to maintain good works.

This is the consistent message of Paul's Pastoral Epistles. Doctrine matters because it produces godly behavior. The Church must have qualified leaders who can teach sound doctrine and refute error. And the believers must live in a way that adorns the gospel and makes it attractive to the watching world.

May we be people who hold fast to sound doctrine and are zealous for good works—not to earn God's favor, but because we have already received it by grace through faith in our great God and Savior, Jesus Christ.

The Pastoral Epistles

Stir It Up
2 Timothy 1:1-7

Paul's second imprisonment is markedly different from his first. During his first imprisonment, recorded in Acts, Paul was under house arrest with relative freedom. He could receive visitors, teach, and even write letters. The Prison Epistles—Ephesians, Philippians, Colossians, and Philemon—all came from that period. At the end of Acts, there is strong indication that Paul was released and continued his ministry.

In Philippians 2:24, Paul writes, "But I trust in the Lord that I myself shall also come shortly." In Philemon 1:22, he asks Philemon to prepare a guest room for him, saying, "For I trust that through your prayers I shall be granted to you." These are not the words of a man expecting execution. Paul anticipated release, and Scripture indicates he was indeed freed and resumed his apostolic work.

But now, as he writes Second Timothy, Paul is back in prison—and this time, it is different. The conditions are harsher. The outlook is grim. Paul knows his time is short. This is his final letter, his last words to his beloved son in the faith, Timothy.

An Apostle by the Will of God

"Paul, an apostle of Jesus Christ by the will of God, according to the promise of life which is in Christ Jesus, to Timothy, a beloved son: Grace, mercy, and peace from

117

God the Father and Christ Jesus our Lord."
(2 Timothy 1:1–2)

Paul opens with his standard greeting, identifying himself as an apostle by the will of God. This is not a title he took for himself or that was bestowed by men. Paul's apostleship came directly from the Lord Jesus Christ on the road to Damascus. It was God's sovereign choice, God's will, that made Paul an apostle.

Notice what his apostleship is according to: "the promise of life which is in Christ Jesus." Paul's entire ministry, his calling, his message—all of it centers on this promise of life. Not temporary, earthly life, but eternal life found only in Jesus Christ. This is the gospel Paul has preached, the truth he has suffered for, and the message he is now passing on to Timothy.

Paul addresses Timothy as "a beloved son." This is deeply personal. Timothy is not just a colleague or a student. He is Paul's son in the faith. Paul loves him. And this letter, written from a dark prison cell with death looming, is a father's final words to his son.

Paul pronounces grace, mercy, and peace upon Timothy from God the Father and Christ Jesus our Lord. These are not empty words. Timothy will need grace for the challenges ahead. He will need mercy as he faces his own weaknesses. And he will need peace—the peace that only God can give—in a world hostile to the gospel.

A Faith Without Hypocrisy

*"I thank God, whom I serve with a pure
conscience, as my forefathers did, as without
ceasing I remember you in my prayers night
and day, greatly desiring to see you, being
mindful of your tears, that I may be filled
with joy, when I call to remembrance the
unfeigned faith that is in you, which dwelt
first in your grandmother Lois and your
mother Eunice, and I am persuaded is in you
also." (2 Timothy 1:3–5)*

Paul begins by expressing his deep gratitude for Timothy.
He serves God with a pure conscience, following in the
footsteps of his forefathers, and he prays for Timothy
constantly—night and day. This is not casual prayer. This
is the prayer of a spiritual father who loves his son and
longs to see him again.

Paul is mindful of Timothy's tears. We do not know the
exact circumstances, but it is clear that Timothy wept at
their last parting. Perhaps he sensed, even then, that he
might not see Paul again. Paul remembers those tears and
desires to see Timothy so that he might be filled with joy.

Then Paul speaks of Timothy's faith. He calls it "unfeigned
faith"—faith without hypocrisy, without pretense. The
word in Greek is *anypokritos* (ἀνυπόκριτος), which means
genuine, sincere, real. This is not a show. This is not a
performance. Timothy's faith is authentic.

119

And this faith has a heritage. It dwelt first in Timothy's grandmother Lois, then in his mother Eunice, and now it is in Timothy. What a beautiful testimony! Here is a family where genuine faith has been passed down from generation to generation. Lois believed. She raised Eunice in the faith. Eunice believed and passed that same faith to Timothy.

Parents and grandparents, do you see the weight of this? The desire to see genuine faith in your children and grandchildren is not just sentimental—it is deeply spiritual. We all have seen people who seemed to have great faith, yet none of their children followed the Lord. But to look down your family tree and see authentic faith being passed from one generation to the next—that is a beautiful thing.

Paul is persuaded that this genuine faith is in Timothy also. He knows Timothy. He has seen his life. He has watched him minister. And he is convinced that Timothy's faith is real.

Rekindle the Fire

> *"Therefore I remind you to stir up the gift of God which is in you through the laying on of my hands." (2 Timothy 1:6)*

Because of this genuine faith Paul knows is in Timothy, he now gives him an important reminder: stir up the gift of God. The word translated "remind" is *anamimnēskō* (ἀναμιμνῄσκω) in Greek. It is more than just a casual reminder. The prefix *ana* means upward or into the midst of. Paul is saying, "Timothy, there is something that was once at the center of your mind, but it has drifted. It has

120

sunk. I want to bring it back up. I want to bring it back to the center."

What is it that needs to be brought back? The gift of God. Timothy received a spiritual gift through the laying on of Paul's hands. We are not told exactly what this gift was, but Paul is telling Timothy that he needs to stir it up.

The Greek word for "stir up" is *anazōpureō* (ἀναζωπυρέω). It only appears here in the New Testament, but it is a vivid word. Breaking it down: *ana* means upward, *zōē* (ζωή) is the word for life, and *pur* (πῦρ) means fire. Put it all together, and you get the idea of rekindling a fire—bringing it upward to make it more alive.

Anyone who has made a fire understands this. At night, the fire burns hot. But by morning, it has died down. There is ash covering the coals. There is no flame. But if you stir up those coals, if you breathe on them, you can take a fire that has grown cold and make it hot again.

That is what Paul is saying. Timothy, you need to be continually stirring up this gift. Notice that Paul is not going to stir it up for Timothy. Paul cannot do that. Timothy has to do it himself. This is an active, ongoing responsibility. The verb is present tense, meaning it is something Timothy must keep doing. He must be actively and continually rekindling this fire.

The Natural Tendency to Drift

Why does Paul need to remind Timothy of this? Because the natural tendency of every believer is to drift. The author

121

of Hebrews puts it plainly: "Therefore we must give the more earnest heed to the things we have heard, lest we drift away" (Hebrews 2:1). Left unattended, a fire grows cold. Left unanchored, a boat drifts away. This is the natural way of things.

We live in a day and age that makes it even harder to keep the fire burning. Jesus warned of this in Matthew 24:10–12, speaking of the last days: "And then many will be offended, will betray one another, and will hate one another. Then many false prophets will rise up and deceive many. And because lawlessness will abound, the love of many will grow cold."

Can you imagine living in a day when many people get offended easily? When trust and respect seem to have no value? When false teachers are everywhere, deceiving many? When lawlessness abounds and love grows cold? We do not have to imagine it. We are living in it. This is the world we face. And Jesus says that because of all this, the love of many will grow cold.

There is a warning here for us. We live in a day when all the junk going on around us has a direct impact on our faith. It seems to want to sap the heat right out of us. It is hard to be an on-fire, zealous Christian when there is so much pulling us down. But what are we called to do? Stir it up. Keep stirring up the coals. If we let them sit there, they will just get colder and colder and colder.

Think about this: you live today. You were not born fifty years ago or a hundred years ago. You live now, in this moment, in this generation. God has made from one blood every nation of men to dwell on the face of the earth, and He has determined their appointed times and the boundaries of their dwellings (Acts 17:26). Every one of us here was intentionally made alive for this day and age. God did not accidentally drop you into the twenty-first century. You were designed for the day in which we live, to face the things we have to face.

But God did not make you ill-equipped. He did not set you up to fail. He designed you for this moment. The problem is that we must be reminded. If this has left the center of your mind, if it has drifted, Paul is bringing it front and center again: you need to be actively kindling this fire, or it is just going to go out. That is the natural way of things.

Consider One Another

Hebrews 10:19–25 gives us practical instruction on how to keep the fire burning:

> *"Therefore, brethren, having boldness to enter the Holiest by the blood of Jesus, by a new and living way which He consecrated for us, through the veil, that is, His flesh, and having a High Priest over the house of God, let us draw near with a true heart in full assurance of faith, having our hearts sprinkled from an evil conscience and our bodies washed with pure water. Let us hold fast the confession of our hope without wavering, for He who promised is faithful. And let us consider one another in order to*

*stir up love and good works, not forsaking
the assembling of ourselves together, as is
the manner of some, but exhorting one
another, and so much the more as you see
the Day approaching."*

Notice the repeated "let us" statements. Let us draw near.
Let us hold fast. Let us consider one another. These are
active commands, things we must choose to do.

First: Let us draw near with a true heart in full assurance of
faith. Because of the blood of Jesus, we have boldness to
enter the Holiest. Our hearts are sprinkled from an evil
conscience. Our bodies are washed with pure water. We are
clean because of Jesus. So draw near.

Second: Let us hold fast the confession of our hope without
wavering, for He who promised is faithful. We are not
holding on because we are strong. We hold on because God
is faithful. He will not let go.

Third: Let us consider one another in order to stir up love
and good works. The word "consider" is *katanoeō*
(κατανοέω) in Greek. It means to fix your mind on
something, to think deeply about it, to give it careful
attention. This is not casual observation. This is intentional
focus.

And it is in the present tense, meaning you keep on doing
it. It is active, meaning you have to do it. And it is
subjunctive mood, meaning it is not automatic—it is a
choice. We are commanded to consider one another. To

look at, think about, and fix our minds on our brothers and sisters in Christ.

Why? In order to stir up love and good works. Here is that stirring-up idea again. We have a job to do. We are to provoke one another, to spur one another on, to poke and prod until love and good works are stirred up. It is almost like you have a job: Look around at your brothers and sisters, consider them, and then go poke that person until you start stirring up love and good works in them.

Some people have truly found their calling in this. Obviously, everyone in every church knows what it is like to have certain people who are particularly good at provoking others—though not always to love and good works!

But then comes verse 25: "Not forsaking the assembling of ourselves together, as is the manner of some." Even two thousand years ago, there were already enough people who did not faithfully join together for church that the writer could say, "as is the manner of some." This is common. Everyone knows there are people who do not regularly come.

But we are told not to forsake the gathering. Why? Because you cannot consider one another if you are not together. You cannot stir up love and good works if you are not present with your brothers and sisters.

Here is a simple truth: If you are tired of being told that you need to be loving, if you are tired of being told to repent of your sins, if you do not want to hear anymore that drunkenness is sin, that you should not be doing drugs, that you should not be cursing or sleeping with someone who is not your spouse, if you are tired of being told you need to work on your anger issues, you are tired of being told to be forgiving and confessing—if you want all this to stop, if you want God to stop speaking to you, there is a solution: forsake the gathering of believers.

When you do not want God to talk, you stop coming to church. And people do that. They get in a funk. They do not like what they are hearing. They know if they show up, someone is going to ask how they are doing and they are going to have to lie. So they forsake The Church.

But it is at church where we consider one another. It is here where we stir up love and good works. We could do better, but it is happening. This is one way we keep the fire kindled.

A Spirit of Power, Love, and a Sound Mind

> *"For God has not given us a spirit of fear,*
> *but of power and of love and of a sound*
> *mind." (2 Timothy 1:7)*

This verse is often quoted, and rightly so. God has not given us a spirit of fear. Fear is not from God. Anxiety, worry, terror—these are not gifts from the Lord. What has He given us? A spirit of power, of love, and of a sound mind.

Power. *Dynamis* (δύναμις) in Greek. This is the word from which we get "dynamite." It is strength, ability, might. God has given you power. Not weakness, not timidity, but power.

Love. *Agapē* (ἀγάπη) in Greek. This is the self-sacrificial love of God. Not emotional sentimentality, but the love that seeks the highest good of another, even at great cost. This is the love God has shown us in Christ, and it is the love He has given us to show others.

A sound mind. *Sōphronismos* (σωφρονισμός) in Greek. This word means self-discipline, self-control, sound judgment. It is the opposite of chaos, confusion, or being out of control. God has given us the ability to think clearly, to exercise discipline, to have sound judgment.

This is what God has given you. Not fear, but power. Not selfishness, but love. Not confusion, but a sound mind. And yet, if we are not actively stirring up the gift God has given us, these things can grow cold. We can drift into fear, into selfishness, into confusion.

This connects to what was said earlier about rekindling the fire. In Titus 2, Paul instructs the older women to teach the younger women, and one of the things they are to teach is to love their husbands and children. Interestingly, the Greek word used there is related to this idea of restoring the mind, bringing it back to the center. The world will wear you out. It will drain the love right out of you. Unless you are actively rekindling, stirring up what God has given you, love—even love for your own family—can grow cold.

The Need for Revival

There is a word for this rekindling of the fire, this stirring up of the coals so that the breath of God breathes upon them and makes them hot again. That word is revival.

Our church is named Revival Bible Church. We are not advertising that we are a church full of people who are perpetually revived. Rather, it is a heart and mindset recognizing that we need revival, and we need it often. I need to be regularly revived by the Lord. I need to be regularly stirring things up. Because I have come to learn that my natural tendency is to drift away, to grow cold, to become complacent.

Unless I am actively engaged in the act of stirring up my faith, stirring up the gift of God that He has given me, it is just going to go away.

Years ago, I went to a men's conference. I was a young believer, just learning, and I did not know who any of these speakers were. There were guys named Jon Courson and Greg Laurie teaching. I had never heard of them. The place was packed. I was sitting in the very front, like I always do.

It was Greg Laurie who made a comment that has stuck with me ever since. He said, "Christianity is like climbing a greased pole. You are either actively trying to climb, or you are sliding downward. It is impossible to just hang on and stay the same. You are actively climbing, or you are going to be sliding downward. Maybe you slide slowly because you have a really tight grip, but the point is, there is no staying still in our faith."

If we are not actively engaged in the act of stirring up those coals, we are going to grow cold. That gift is going to be unused. And many, many people will not be blessed because of the blessing they were supposed to receive through you and the ministry God has given you.

Brought Back to Remembrance

A few years ago, a friend sent me a video clip from years past—us worshiping together, singing about the love of God and our love for Him. It was a beautiful thing. All they said was, "I just want to get my heart back to here."

I get that. So much. Many of us need to be brought back to remembrance. There is something we used to know, something we used to feel, that needs to be brought back up and brought to the center of attention. We need to rekindle a fire. We need to stir it up.

It is an act of choice. It is not just going to happen. There will be drifting and distancing unless we are active about this.

It is hard. That is why you need to get stubborn—in a good kind of way.

In Genesis 32:26, the angel of the Lord tells Jacob, "Let Me go, for the day breaks." But Jacob says, "I will not let You go unless You bless me!" That is the kind of attitude some of us need. "I am praying and I am not feeling it. Well, Lord, I am getting stubborn. I am just going to keep on praying until You bless me. I am not going anywhere. I want to hear from You, God."

In John 6, Jesus says to the Twelve, "Do you also want to go away?" Peter answers, "Lord, to whom shall we go? You have the words of eternal life."

In Mark 6:48, Jesus is walking on the sea and "would have passed them by." They had to summon Him into the boat. In Luke 24:28, on the road to Emmaus, Jesus "indicated that He would have gone farther." They had to ask Him to stay.

It seems like God gives us many opportunities to request His presence, to request His help. He gives us the opportunity to stray sometimes so we can see how authentic our determination and love for Him really is.

Many of us need to be brought back to remembrance. We need to stir up the gift God has given us. We need to gather together often. We need to consider one another and spur one another on to love and good works. We need to walk in the spirit of power, love, and a sound mind that He has given us.

There is no standing still. We are either climbing or sliding. We are either stirring up the coals or watching them grow cold. May God help us to be people who actively and continually rekindle the fire, who refuse to let go until He blesses us, who draw near and hold fast and consider one another.

In the next section, Paul builds on this foundation with a charge to Timothy: Do not be ashamed of the testimony of the Lord.

Fit for the Master's Use
2 Timothy 1:8–2:26

The Gospel and Suffering (1:8–14)

In the previous section, Paul reminded Timothy of his sincere faith and called him to stir up the gift of God within him. He emphasized that God has not given us a spirit of fear, but of power, love, and a sound mind. Now Paul builds on that foundation with a direct charge.

> *"Therefore do not be ashamed of the testimony of our Lord, nor of me His prisoner, but share with me in the sufferings for the gospel according to the power of God."* (2 Timothy 1:8)

Because believers possess this power, this encouragement, they need not be ashamed of the gospel or of those who suffer for it. Paul invites Timothy to share in the sufferings that accompany faithful gospel ministry. This is an important acknowledgment: following Christ will involve hardship. It helps when believers know this ahead of time, rather than being told one thing and experiencing something entirely different.

Jesus Himself prepared His disciples for this reality. In John 16, He tells them plainly:

> *"These things I have spoken to you, that you should not be made to stumble. They will put you out of the synagogues; yes, the time is coming that whoever kills you will think that he offers God service. And these things they will do to you because they have not known the Father nor Me. But these things I*

131

have told you, that when the time comes, you may
remember that I told you of them." (John 16:1–4)

Jesus wanted His followers to know hard times were
coming. In the same way, Paul tells Timothy: expect
resistance. If believers are living out the gospel in an
unbelieving world that opposes it, there will be friction.
Sometimes it is painful resistance—when people you love
decide they no longer want to hear from you because you
care about their soul. This warning prepares believers for
the reality of gospel ministry.

The Gospel Defined

Paul continues by describing the gospel itself:

> *"...who has saved us and called us with a holy*
> *calling, not according to our works, but according*
> *to His own purpose and grace which was given to*
> *us in Christ Jesus before time began."*
> (2 Timothy 1:9)

This is another one of the great verses emphasizing that
salvation comes by grace, not works. Paul wrote similarly
to the Ephesians:

> *"For by grace you have been saved through faith,*
> *and that not of yourselves; it is the gift of God, not*
> *of works, lest anyone should boast."*
> (Ephesians 2:8–9)

Paul mentions that this grace was given "before time
began." How does that work? Revelation 13:8 refers to
Jesus as "the Lamb slain from the foundation of the world."
Understanding this requires grasping the timelessness of
God. Genesis opens with "In the beginning God created the
heavens and the earth." Those words "in the beginning"

mark the start of time itself. Eternity is not simply a long duration before and after—heaven will not be "a long time" but rather timeless. Before time began, time did not exist. God simply existed outside of time.

This is difficult for time-bound creatures to comprehend. We only know time. When someone tries to explain "no time," how can the mind even process that? Heaven without a sun—how does that work? Our brains struggle with such concepts.

Now combine God's timelessness with His omniscience. God knows everything and has known everything from the beginning. God knew how every sermon would unfold, word for word, before time began. He knew what each person would do this afternoon. He also knew everyone who would choose Him and everyone who would reject Him. Before time began, God knew He would need to save this lost world, and therefore it was predetermined—Jesus Christ was as good as crucified before time began. That is why Paul can speak of grace "given to us in Christ Jesus before time began." God knew this was always going to be the plan.

Jesus said to His disciples, "You did not choose Me, but I chose you" (John 15:16). While that statement applied directly to the disciples' calling, it serves as a reminder for all believers. Sometimes two camps of people want to fight over whether humans choose God or God chooses them. The answer is yes—both are true. The Bible clearly presents the command to choose: "Choose for yourselves this day whom you will serve" (Joshua 24:15). There are commands throughout Scripture to decide to follow the Lord. But that decision has been known to God before time began. God entered creation knowing everyone who would choose Him and everyone who would not. From the moment a person is born, God already knows whether they are one of His.

These truths can be difficult to wrestle with. But studying the character of God actually opens many doors. Rather than focusing narrowly on the present, stepping back to consider God's eternal nature helps everything fall into place. Yet just because God knew what would happen does not mean He removed the choice. God's foreknowledge and human free will are not mutually exclusive—they both exist simultaneously.

Paul speaks of this gospel as a holy calling, given in Christ before time began. God always had this plan. But here is the difference: this plan has always been in motion, but it has now been revealed.

> *"...but has now been revealed by the appearing of our Savior Jesus Christ, who has abolished death and brought life and immortality to light through the gospel."* (2 Timothy 1:10)

Now believers can see this plan in action. It has been revealed by Christ's appearing. The word "appearing" is significant—it shows up mostly in the Pastoral Epistles. Six out of seven New Testament uses occur in these letters. It became a word Paul used more and more toward the end of his life. Paul wrote to Titus:

> *"...looking for the blessed hope and glorious appearing of our great God and Savior Jesus Christ."* (Titus 2:13)

The Greek word is *epiphaneia* (ἐπιφάνεια), from which we get the English word "epiphany"—when something suddenly dawns on a person, when understanding hits. Christ appeared in His first coming, but He will appear again. That second appearing is something believers eagerly anticipate.

Paul says Jesus "abolished death." This does not mean no one physically dies anymore—that is obviously not the case. But twofold, because of Jesus believers have eternal life, and more significantly, there is no longer any fear in death. Paul makes this point powerfully in 1 Corinthians:

> *"O Death, where is your sting? O Hades, where is your victory?"* (1 Corinthians 15:55)

It is good to recognize that the process of dying may not be pleasant—that is not something to look forward to. But death itself, the moment of passing, no longer holds terror for the believer. Jesus has taken the sting and pain out of death. He has abolished it. Christians need not worry about what comes after because they know they will be in His presence. As Paul told the Thessalonians, believers are not "like those who have no hope" (1 Thessalonians 4:13). Going to be with the Lord is a glorious thing, something to be thankful for and to anticipate.

Paul's Commitment

> *"...to which I was appointed a preacher, an apostle, and a teacher of the Gentiles. For this reason I also suffer these things; nevertheless I am not ashamed, for I know whom I have believed and am persuaded that He is able to keep what I have committed to Him until that Day."* (2 Timothy 1:11–12)

The phrase "to keep what I have committed to Him" has generated different interpretations throughout church history. Scholars have debated what exactly Paul meant. Some suggest Paul is speaking of his life, his ministry, his converts, or his heavenly reward. The exact meaning cannot be determined with certainty, but the principle is clear: Paul has entrusted something precious to God, and he is confident God will preserve it.

George Mueller provides a beautiful illustration of this principle. After like 60, it's like 60 years of praying for, the guy comes to know the Lord just like within half a year or so before he dies. Number five comes to the Lord months after he dies. But he prayed a lifetime for these men to come to know the Lord. And God kept what George Mueller had committed to him.

Hold Fast to Sound Words

> *"Hold fast the pattern of sound words which you have heard from me, in faith and love which are in Christ Jesus. That good thing which was committed to you, keep by the Holy Spirit who dwells in us."* (2 Timothy 1:13–14)

Paul laid down a pattern for Timothy to follow. He wrote to the Corinthians, "Imitate me, just as I also imitate Christ" (1 Corinthians 11:1). Paul could say with all boldness: just do what I have been doing and you will do well.

Paul reminds Timothy that the Holy Spirit enables this faithfulness. The same Spirit who dwelt in Paul dwells in Timothy—the same Spirit who raised Jesus from the dead. That power is available to every believer.

Faithful Friends

> *"This you know, that all those in Asia have turned away from me, among whom are Phygelus and Hermogenes. The Lord grant mercy to the household of Onesiphorus, for he often refreshed*

me, and was not ashamed of my chain; but when he arrived in Rome, he sought me out very zealously and found me." (2 Timothy 1:15–17)

Paul mentions that many in Asia had abandoned him— including Phygelus and Hermogenes, about whom little else is known. But Onesiphorus stands out as a faithful friend. The text emphasizes that he "sought me out very zealously and found me," implying it was not easy to locate Paul.

This detail makes sense when understanding Paul's circumstances. During his first imprisonment recorded in Acts, Paul was under a relatively comfortable house arrest. He had been arrested on a Jewish technicality and, as a Roman citizen, appealed to Caesar. The centurions allowed him considerable freedom—he took shore leave, had soldiers accompany him, and when he arrived in Rome, he stayed in decent accommodations. People came and went freely to see him.

But this second imprisonment was different. Between the writing of Titus and Second Timothy, Paul was arrested again—this time as a leader of what Nero had declared an illegal religion. Now Paul was a condemned criminal, held in a dungeon. Tradition identifies this as the Mamertine Prison, where prisoners were kept in lower levels under harsh conditions. Peter was likely imprisoned there around the same time. In this context, Onesiphorus's determination to find Paul and minister to him becomes even more remarkable and precious.

Faithful Men and Practical Examples (2:1–7)

> *"You therefore, my son, be strong in the grace that is in Christ Jesus. And the things that you have heard from me among many witnesses, commit these to faithful men who will be able to teach others also."* (2 Timothy 2:1–2)

This charge remains desperately needed in the Church today. There are two types of advice often given. One is that pastors need to replicate themselves. The other is that they need to raise up people who are nothing like themselves. Both contain truth. The church needs diversity of gifts and ministries—not just ministries that look identical. But there is also a need for replication, where those who have been taught continue teaching what they have learned.

Paul gives Timothy three practical illustrations from daily life to drive this point home.

As a Soldier

> *"You therefore must endure hardship as a good soldier of Jesus Christ. No one engaged in warfare entangles himself with the affairs of this life, that he may please him who enlisted him as a soldier."* (2 Timothy 2:3–4)

Soldiers endure hardships. Perhaps some who enlist in the military do not fully realize what they are signing up for, but few people join the Marines, show up at basic training, and express shock that they have to run. People understand that soldiers train hard and do difficult things.

138

Paul tells Timothy: you are a Christian, you have signed on to do hard things. Some of what God calls believers to will not be easy. Jesus spoke about this in Luke 9, emphasizing the cost of discipleship. He concluded:

"No one, having put his hand to the plow, and looking back, is fit for the kingdom of God." (Luke 9:62)

Jesus is saying: if you want to do this, do it. Get in the game. Do not sit there looking back at your old life. Recognize that you have signed on for something demanding.

Verse 4 can be summarized as: soldiers belong to their own culture now. Anyone who has military family or close friends who have served knows this. Once people join the military, something changes in them. They dramatically change when they enlist. They become part of a different culture with different priorities and different concerns.

The Greek word for "entangle" is *emplekō* (ἐμπλέκω), meaning to interweave or braid together. The soldier cannot become woven into civilian pursuits while trying to serve in the military. In the same way, Christians are not to be entangled with the things of this world in ways that compromise their service to Christ.

The unbelieving world is not concerned about lost souls. They are not thinking about using their time effectively for the Lord. But believers know that the Lord Jesus could return at any moment, and when He comes back, there will be no more praying, no more evangelism, no more opportunities. Like good soldiers, Christians must use their time effectively.

As an Athlete

> *"And also if anyone competes in athletics, he is not crowned unless he competes according to the rules."* (2 Timothy 2:5)

Several principles emerge from this illustration. First, there is the word "competes"—believers are in a competition. This is not a relaxed endeavor where one can simply show up and stand around. Active involvement and effort are required.

Second, athletes must compete according to the rules. This is obvious in sports—breaking the rules results in penalties or disqualification. The Christian life also has rules. Not merely moral laws, but principles of sowing and reaping:

> *"Do not be deceived, God is not mocked; for whatever a man sows, that he will also reap."* (Galatians 6:7)

Paul uses this same principle regarding giving in 2 Corinthians: those who sow liberally will reap liberally; those who sow sparingly will reap sparingly. This is a general principle of God's economy. Christians play by different rules than the world, but they are still rules that must be followed.

Consider giving, for example. God calls different people to give differently. But once a person has peace about what God has called them to give, neglecting that brings consequences. The Bible addresses this directly. Or consider:

> *"Do not be unequally yoked together with unbelievers. For what fellowship has righteousness with lawlessness? And what communion has light with darkness?"* (2 Corinthians 6:14)

Christians know one who is a marginal Christian, who begins dating an unbeliever, and suddenly that unbeliever claims conversion in order to date the person. Then two years into marriage comes the admission: "I never really was a Christian." This happens frequently. The Bible gives clear instructions as warnings because God loves His people and wants to protect them from pain and heartache. If you are an athlete and you know the rules, play by the rules. Doing what God says will turn out far better.

Third, athletes compete to be crowned. Paul wrote to the Corinthians:

> *"Do you not know that those who run in a race all run, but one receives the prize? Run in such a way that you may obtain it. And everyone who competes for the prize is temperate in all things. Now they do it to obtain a perishable crown, but we for an imperishable crown."* (1 Corinthians 9:24–25)

I was a wrestler. I trained all the time. I was tempered in all things—I watched what I ate. I remember a kid once offered me a cookie, and I told him no thanks. He looked surprised, but I explained I was watching my weight for wrestling. The mindset was: I am in this to win it. That should be the Christian mindset as well.

As a Farmer

> *"The hardworking farmer must be first to partake of the crops."* (2 Timothy 2:6)

This verse has generated different interpretations. One understanding is this: no one will buy produce from a farmer who has never tasted his own crops. "Are they good apples?" "I don't know, I've never tried them." People want to receive from someone who can speak from experience.

In the same way, believers cannot infect others with something they have not caught themselves. If believers want to win people to Jesus, they need to be living a life worth catching, worth sharing. They must partake of the wonderful gospel they are trying to share. They need to experience it, not just give mental assent to it.

Paul then instructs Timothy:

> *"Consider what I say, and may the Lord give you understanding in all things."* (2 Timothy 2:7)

These illustrations require meditation. The Lord will grant understanding to those who consider them carefully.

Fixing Our Eyes on Jesus (2:8–13)

> *"Remember that Jesus Christ, of the seed of David, was raised from the dead according to my gospel, for which I suffer trouble as an evildoer, even to the point of chains; but the word of God is not chained."* (2 Timothy 2:8–9)

Paul shifts focus to Jesus Himself. The reminder is simple: remember Jesus Christ, risen from the dead. Paul suffers for this gospel—he is treated as a criminal, even to the point of chains. But then comes this triumphant declaration: "the word of God is not chained."

Paul may be in chains, but the word of God is getting out and accomplishing its purpose. Nothing can stop it. Spurgeon once made a similar point: the word of God does not need to be defended like some fragile thing. It is like a lion—just open the cage and let it loose.

> *"Therefore I endure all things for the sake of the elect, that they also may obtain the salvation which*

142

is in Christ Jesus with eternal glory."
(2 Timothy 2:10)

Paul's mindset is clear: he will endure anything for the gospel. It does not matter what he goes through. He wrote similarly to the Corinthians about becoming all things to all people that he might by all means save some (1 Corinthians 9:19–23). Paul had this disposition of being willing to suffer anything, take anything, endure chains, endure death—if it promotes the gospel.

What a beautiful example. Paul does not care about his preferences or his comfort. He cares that people get saved and God gets glorified. That is what matters.

A Faithful Saying

Verse 11 begins with "This is a faithful saying." As noted in earlier chapters, only the Pastoral Epistles contain this phrase. These were among the last books Paul wrote, and these "faithful sayings" appear to have been well-known teachings in the early church—possibly even hymns that congregations sang together.

> *"For if we died with Him, we shall also live with Him. If we endure, we shall also reign with Him. If we deny Him, He also will deny us. If we are faithless, He remains faithful; He cannot deny Himself."* (2 Timothy 2:11–13)

"If we died with Him, we shall also live with Him." This echoes the imagery of baptism—buried with Christ but raised to newness of life. When a person becomes a believer, they die to this world and die with Christ, knowing they will live with Him.

143

"If we endure, we shall also reign with Him." This relates to heavenly rewards. Different positions will be given to those who have endured well—like the servants in Jesus' parable who were faithful with little and were put in charge of cities. There is reward for enduring.

"If we deny Him, He also will deny us." This recalls Jesus' words:

> *"But whoever denies Me before men, him I will also deny before My Father who is in heaven."*
> (Matthew 10:33)

This is straightforward. Those who reject Jesus will stand before the Great White Throne judgment without an advocate. Jesus will not intercede for those who denied Him on earth. That is how it works—this life is the opportunity to surrender to Him.

"If we are faithless, He remains faithful." Here is the key distinction. To *deny* Him is a willful, intentional denial. To be *faithless* refers to passive weakness or fault—stumbling, not doing what one knows they should, failing due to human frailty.

The beautiful truth is this: even when believers stumble, even when they fail through weakness, God remains faithful. He cannot deny Himself. His character does not change.

Scripture testifies to this throughout:

> *"He remembers His covenant forever, the word which He commanded, for a thousand generations."*
> (Psalm 105:8)

> *"Jesus Christ is the same yesterday, today, and forever."* (Hebrews 13:8)

James writes that God is the "Father of lights, with whom there is no variation or shadow of turning" (James 1:17). There is not even a hint of Him changing. God was faithful at the beginning; He will be faithful at the end. If a believer has ever felt the sensation of God's love, it is still there and has not changed.

Even in the sorrowful book of Lamentations, this truth shines:

> *"Through the LORD's mercies we are not consumed, because His compassions fail not. They are new every morning; great is Your faithfulness."*
> (Lamentations 3:22–23)

This is a beautiful little hymn. God cannot deny Himself. His faithfulness remains even when ours wavers.

Approved and Disapproved Workers (2:14–26)

> *"Remind them of these things, charging them before the Lord not to strive about words to no profit, to the ruin of the hearers."* (2 Timothy 2:14)

Paul returns to a theme he has addressed multiple times in the Pastoral Epistles: the danger of fruitless disputes. In the ancient world without internet, printing press, or mass communication, ideas spread primarily through oral transmission. False teachers operated by talking—engaging people in debates and discussions that led nowhere profitable. Their arguments ruined those who listened.

Rightly Dividing the Word

"Be diligent to present yourself approved to God, a worker who does not need to be ashamed, rightly dividing the word of truth." (2 Timothy 2:15)

This is good stuff—a verse every believer should highlight.

The word translated "be diligent" (or "study" in the King James) is *spoudazō* (σπουδάζω). It is translated various ways: diligent, diligence, endeavor, be forward, labor, study. The word means to hasten, to be eager, and also to exert oneself.

Here is what makes this word significant: it captures both attitude and action—an inward disposition and an outward effort. English typically picks one or the other, but the Greek encompasses both. "Being diligent" captures the attitude—zealous, eager, committed. "Studying" captures the action—because rightly dividing the word requires actual study. That is why the King James translators chose "study." The newer translations say "be diligent" because that is also what the word means. Really, "study diligently" captures the full meaning: study diligently to present yourself approved.

The phrase "rightly dividing" translates *orthotomeō* (ὀρθοτομέω), which literally means to cut straight or evenly. In the Greek world, this word had various applications. A cook would make straight and even portions to give everyone equal servings. A farmer would plow straight and even rows. The idea is precision and consistency when making something uniform.

Applied to Scripture, this means being able to work through the word of God, understand it, and keep it in context. When someone quotes a verse, the person who rightly divides can recognize whether that interpretation aligns

146

with the rest of Scripture. They can take all the verses together and make sense of them all.

Jesus challenged the Pharisees four times with the question, "Have you not read?" The Pharisees were supposed to be the Bible experts, so asking them "Have you not read?" was deeply insulting. But Jesus asked it repeatedly because they had failed to rightly divide the word.

In Acts 17, the Bereans are commended:

> *"These were more fair-minded than those in Thessalonica, in that they received the word with all readiness, and searched the Scriptures daily to find out whether these things were so."* (Acts 17:11)

They heard Paul preach and then went home to check whether his teaching aligned with Scripture. That is the model—hearing teaching, then searching the Scriptures to verify it.

"Straight Outta Context"

Taking Scripture out of context is typically not a joking matter, but some humorous examples help illustrate the danger.

For single ladies, you might cling to Matthew 16:24, "If any man desires to come after me, let him...." And if you don't like the guy, then Romans 1:13, "I would not have you... ignorant brethren...."

Here is a verse we could quote for voting: Ecclesiastes 10:2, "A wise man's heart inclines him toward the right, but a fool's heart toward the left."

For those who are not morning people: Isaiah 5:11 declares, "Woe to those who rise early in the morning." (Though the verse continues, "that they may follow intoxicating drink.")

For oldest children: Proverbs 17:17 says, "A sibling is born for adversity." Every oldest child feels vindicated—life was good until that younger sibling came along!

Here is a good prosperity verse: "If you will worship before me, all will be yours" (Luke 4:7). The problem? That was Satan who said that to Jesus during the temptation.

Consider this seemingly inspirational verse: "For this very purpose I have raised you up, that I may show My power in you, and that My name may be declared in all the earth" (Romans 9:17). That sounds wonderful until one realizes God is speaking to Pharaoh—He raised Pharaoh up specifically to knock him down and demonstrate His power. Context matters!

Prosperity Gospel preacher Jesse Duplantis once quoted Psalms 49:16 in a broadcast: "Be not afraid when one is made rich, when the glory of his house is increased." He used this as a proof text for prosperity teaching and to justify his jet he had bought. But his wife, reading along in the Amplified Bible, saw what came next: "Be not afraid when an ungodly one is made rich." The verse is actually saying God does not care whether godly or ungodly people are rich—it makes no difference whatsoever because when they die, they carry nothing away. Her eyes grew wide as she read the context that contradicted his point.

This is exactly the problem Paul is addressing. If Duplantis's wife had not read, viewers might have simply accepted his interpretation. But when she read it cleared everything up and made him look like a fool. Teachers of Scripture must do better than grabbing isolated phrases.

Shun Profane Babblings

> *"But shun profane and idle babblings, for they will increase to more ungodliness. And their message will spread like cancer, of which Hymenaeus and Philetus are of this sort, who have strayed concerning the truth, saying that the resurrection is already past; and they overthrow the faith of some."* (2 Timothy 2:16–18)

Paul commands Timothy to shun these empty arguments and silence them before they spread. The word translated "cancer" is *gangraina* (γάγγραινα)—literally, gangrene. This disease causes inflammation that spreads through the body, corrupting healthy tissue. Unless it is cut off and the wound treated carefully, it spreads until it kills. In old wartime movies, soldiers have limbs amputated precisely because of gangrene—the only way to save the patient was to remove the infected part before it spread everywhere.

False teaching operates the same way. Unless it is cut out, it spreads through the church body and destroys faith.

Paul specifically names Hymenaeus and Philetus, who taught that the resurrection had already occurred. Some today hold similar views under what is called "full preterism"—the belief that Jesus has already returned spiritually and now reigns through the Church, that all biblical prophecy has been fulfilled, and the world will simply continue indefinitely. The early church condemned this as heresy, and Paul does the same here. Teaching that the resurrection is past overthrows the faith of some.

The Solid Foundation

> *"Nevertheless the solid foundation of God stands, having this seal: 'The Lord knows those who are*

> *His,' and, 'Let everyone who names the name of*
> *Christ depart from iniquity.'"* (2 Timothy 2:19)

Despite the false teachers and their destructive doctrines,
God's foundation remains firm. The Lord knows who truly
belongs to Him—these false teachers are not His. The word
of God will stand. True believers will not ultimately be
swept away by such errors.

Vessels of Honor

> *"But in a great house there are not only vessels of*
> *gold and silver, but also of wood and clay, some for*
> *honor and some for dishonor. Therefore if anyone*
> *cleanses himself from the latter, he will be a vessel*
> *for honor, sanctified and useful for the Master,*
> *prepared for every good work."* (2 Timothy 2:20–
> 21)

The word "sanctified" is from *hagiazō* (ἁγιάζω), and "holy"
simply means set apart. God is perfectly holy—perfectly
set apart from sin. Believers are called to be holy, to be set
apart from sin.

Do you want to be holy? Then be set apart.

Some people have fine china or special silverware that is
only used for special occasions. I remember in college we
ate on paper plates. But when people came over that we
were trying to impress, we got out the Chinet—the hard
paper plates, the good stuff. That is the idea: having
something special, set apart for a particular purpose.

Believers are called to be set apart, not called to be like
everyone else. In Acts 13, the Holy Spirit told the church at
Antioch: "Now separate to Me Barnabas and Saul for the

150

work to which I have called them" (Acts 13:2). God had a special calling for those men—they were to be set apart.

Paul identifies four characteristics of a vessel of honor. First, it is sanctified—set apart. Second, it is useful (or "fit" in the King James). F.B. Meyer wrote a beautiful book on this passage called "Fit for the Master's Use." He began with an appeal for each person to examine themselves lest God cease to use them because of sin. Just like a wrench that does not quite fit the bolt—you might shove it in there and get the job done, but it was not the right tool. The vessel that fits is the one God reaches for.

You might not be the sharpest tool in the drawer, but if you are near the Lord, He will most definitely use you.

Third, the vessel is prepared. There are many tools that must be prepared before use. Believers should want to be ready when God calls. One of the first sermons I ever gave, I quoted Winston Churchill:

"To each there comes in their lifetime a special moment when they are figuratively tapped on the shoulder and offered the chance to do a very special thing, unique to them and fitted to their talents. What a tragedy if that moment finds them unprepared or unqualified for that which could have been their finest hour."

That is sobering in a positive sense—but there is also a warning. Every day presents an opportunity to disqualify oneself. Paul wrote:

> *"But I discipline my body and bring it into*
> *subjection, lest, when I have preached to others, I*
> *myself should become disqualified."* (1 Corinthians
> 9:27)

Everyone knows what tempts them. If put in a place where that temptation is present, do not flirt with it—flee from it. If something tempting is in the vicinity, run away.

The Servant of the Lord

> *"Flee also youthful lusts; but pursue righteousness, faith, love, peace with those who call on the Lord out of a pure heart."* (2 Timothy 2:22)

"Pursue" is the key word. The idea is not merely avoiding evil but actively chasing after righteousness, faith, love, and peace. And notice: "with those who call on the Lord out of a pure heart." Pursue these things together with other believers.

When I was a young believer, I surrounded myself with Christians. It had a dramatic impact on my walk. Being surrounded by people—some of whom were only a few steps ahead of me in their faith—made all the difference. My good friend had only been a believer a little while longer than I had, but it was enough. We were always together, sharpening each other, challenging each other, holding each other accountable. Christian friends help you flee lust and pursue faith, love, and peace.

My pastor once said: it is one thing to surround yourself with people who call themselves Christians; it is another thing to surround yourself with genuinely godly people. Do not settle for less. Get around people who will inspire growth.

> *"But avoid foolish and ignorant disputes, knowing that they generate strife. And a servant of the Lord must not quarrel but be gentle to all, able to teach, patient, in humility correcting those who are in opposition, if God perhaps will grant them*

152

repentance, so that they may know the truth, and that they may come to their senses and escape the snare of the devil, having been taken captive by him to do his will." (2 Timothy 2:23–26)

Paul lists the characteristics required of the Lord's servant: gentle, able to teach, patient, and humble.

Do not think of gentleness as weakness. Gentleness is strength under control. Interestingly, the only adjective Jesus uses to describe Himself in the Gospels is "meek" (Matthew 11:29)—He calls Himself meek. Meekness means keeping power under control, being careful with situations and people because you are paying attention.

Being "able to teach" is significant. That Greek phrase shows up in only two places: here and in 1 Timothy 3 among the qualifications for overseers. This is not just for professional teachers—it applies to everyone who wants to serve. All believers are supposed to be correcting people, training people, making disciples. That is all teaching. And one cannot teach what they do not know. One will not know well if they do not study. This all builds on what came before.

Even sharing the gospel is teaching. A person cannot present the gospel without teaching—teaching that people are sinners, teaching that there is a God, teaching that there is a way back to Him.

The goal of this gentle, patient teaching is that opponents might repent. "Repentance" (*metanoia*) does not mean a change of actions—it means a change of mind. When the mind truly changes, actions follow. If a person truly believes something, their actions will flow from that belief. But the transformation begins in the mind.

Finally, notice the posture Paul prescribes. Believers should not be angry with those in opposition—they should pity them. These people have been deceived by Satan. They are captives doing his will. Perhaps someone is spouting views that make you angry—whether it is promoting abortion, advocating for a false religion, or making atheistic claims. Remember: at the end of the day, this poor person is deceived by Satan. They will pay for it in eternity in hell if they do not repent, if they do not have that change of mind to stop believing what they currently believe and believe on the Lord.

That reality should move believers to humble, gentle, patient teaching—not angry quarreling. The servant of the Lord corrects in humility, hoping God will grant repentance so that the captive might escape the devil's snare.

Paul's Grand Finale
2 Timothy 3-4

Perilous Times Will Come

Paul the Apostle opens this section with a warning—not just for Timothy, but for the entire church:

> *"But know this, that in the last days perilous times will come." (2 Timothy 3:1)*

This warning bears repeating. These are things believers should know. This should not be surprising. It should not catch The Church off guard. Biblical Christians should know that in the last days, perilous times will come.

It is worth noting that the phrase "last days" has been used throughout the entire Christian era. If this warning only applied to Christians in the final generation before Christ's return, it would have had no application to Timothy himself. It had to apply to Timothy and to believers today. Since the birth of The Church, history has unfolded like birth pangs—seasons of greater apostasy followed by darker times, then revivals that lifted The Church out of decline. Even The Church in America alone has experienced dark seasons punctuated by revivals: the First Great Awakening, the Second Great Awakening, the Azusa Street Revival, and the Jesus Movement in the last 150 years. There have been ebbs and flows, ups and downs. But as history moves toward the great apostasy of the end times—where things will be most perilous of all—believers must know that difficult times are coming.

The word "perilous" is the Greek *chalepos* (χαλεπός), meaning hard to do, hard to bear, troublesome, unbearable, or impassable. This word appears only here and in Matthew 8:28, where it describes the demon-possessed man Legion—someone so dangerous that no one could pass by him. The word conveys something almost impossible to handle. Perilous times are coming that will be extraordinarily difficult to endure. Believers need to know this.

The Character of Perilous Times

> *"For men will be lovers of themselves, lovers of money, boasters, proud, blasphemers, disobedient to parents, unthankful, unholy, unloving, unforgiving, slanderers..." (2 Timothy 3:2-3)*

Paul now describes the people of these times. On this list are numerous attitudes that every believer must recognize, because Satan and his minions would love to trap any Christian with even one of them. How many vices does it take to derail a Christian walk? Just one. A single foothold can sink the ship if it goes unchecked.

Lovers of Themselves

"Men will be lovers of themselves" (2 Timothy 3:2). This is the root cause from which everything else flows. Self-love is the opposite of the spirit of Christ. God is *agape*— sacrificial love. These last days will be summarized by people who love themselves above all else.

> *"For even the Son of Man did not come to be served, but to serve, and to give His life a ransom for many." (Mark 10:45)*

This verse encapsulates the ministry of Jesus Christ. He came to serve and love others. Yet believers today live in a time when Satan uses every tool available to turn hearts inward—toward personal needs, preferences, and desires. This self-focus manifests in many destructive ways.

Lovers of Money

As discussed in the chapter on 1 Timothy 6, being rich is not a sin, but the love of money is a root from which every form of evil can spring. Because of the love of money, people become unfaithful. Because of the love of money, people cheat. Because of the love of money, people commit sexual immorality. It is remarkable how the love of money can lead into every kind of trouble.

Boasters, Proud, and Blasphemers

These three belong together. People who love themselves will be quick to boast, and that boasting flows from pride. As anyone who has observed human nature knows, those who love themselves do not merely talk themselves up— they also tear others down. The Greek word *blasphemia* (βλασφημία) can be used more broadly than blasphemy against God specifically. In this broader context, it means tearing other people down through destructive speech. Those who love themselves exalt themselves while denigrating others.

Disobedient to Parents

A friend of mine who does parenting workshops once read through this list (or the similar one in Romans 1) and asked his audience what was missing. Many did not catch it: disobedience to parents sits right in the middle of this grotesque catalog of sins. Romans 1:30 lists "backbiters, haters of God, violent, proud, boasters, inventors of evil things, disobedient to parents"—placing haters of God and disobedience to parents side by side.

If God commands children to obey their parents in the Lord, then those under their parents' authority must be obedient. When children grow up, marry, and leave home, they still honor their parents for the rest of their lives— even if obedience in the same sense no longer applies. Why do teenagers begin to disobey their parents? It comes back to love of self. As they grow older, they want to become their own person, to do things their own way. Parents are usually the primary obstacle between teenagers and everything they want. This is why disobedience to parents flows so naturally from self-love.

Believers should know that in the last days, difficult times will come—and disobedience to parents will be increasingly visible in society. This is already apparent, and it is no surprise when The Church adopts the world's parenting methods and standards rather than the Lord's.

Unthankful

This is a sin. It would not be on the list otherwise. Unthankful people are complainers. When someone is thankful for all things—recognizing that every good and perfect gift comes from the Lord—gratitude flows naturally. But when thankfulness is absent, complaining rushes in to fill the void.

> *"Do all things without complaining and disputing." (Philippians 2:14)*

> *"Nor complain, as some of them also complained [in the Wilderness], and were destroyed by the destroyer." (1 Corinthians 10:10)*

158

Complaining in the Bible is a sin. In the last days, as people love themselves more and more, they will complain constantly because they are unthankful, believing they deserve better than they have: "I am not being treated the way I deserve. I am not getting what I deserve." This is challenging material—it strikes at the heart. It is one thing to say Christians should avoid obvious vices, but quite another to examine these heart issues that reveal whether the heart of Christ dwells within.

Unholy and Unloving

"Unholy" is broad in scope. "Unloving" translates *astorgoi* (ἄστοργοι), which the King James Version renders as "without natural affection." This is *storge* love—the natural family bond—negated by the alpha privative. *Storge* is the love that appears instantaneously when a baby is born. It is the natural bond within families.

In the last days, this natural love will diminish. Fathers will not care about their children. Mothers will abandon their own kids. Is this not increasingly visible with each passing generation? This is a sign of the times—when even natural family affection fades away. May this never happen in The Church, where believers are called to love one another. Yet if people struggle to love their own mothers, fathers, sons, and daughters, the challenge becomes even greater.

Unforgiving

A sign of the end times that believers should know well is that people will struggle with forgiveness. If anyone is holding onto a grudge, that person is in sin. That is what the Bible teaches. Grudges cannot be held. If bitterness is permitted to dwell within, it puts the entire church in jeopardy:

159

> *"...lest any root of bitterness springing up cause trouble, and by this many become defiled." (Hebrews 12:15)*

Personal sin of unforgiveness breeds bitterness, and bitterness spreads. A bitter person thrown into a group of Christians affects others. Someone in a bad mood can affect everyone's mood. It is a reminder that unforgiveness is the root—and if believers forgive their transgressors and ask God to forgive them as they forgive their debtors, bitterness will not take hold. Choosing unforgiveness means choosing to embrace bitterness.

Slanderers

"Slanderers" is *diabolos* (διάβολος)—the same word translated "devil" thirty-five times in the New Testament and "slanderer" three times. The devil is the slanderer; this is what he does. He tears people down. Related words appear in Romans 1: "whisperers" (*psithyristēs*, a gossiper or secret slanderer) and "backbiters" (*katalalos*, literally "talkative against"). A slanderer speaks publicly; a whisperer murmurs in secret. Both tear others down.

Believers must watch their mouths. This kind of talk can tear down an entire church. When someone begins speaking this way, the Holy Spirit must provide power to lovingly but firmly say, "We cannot have this."

> *"These six things the LORD hates, yes, seven are an abomination to Him: a proud look, a lying tongue, hands that shed innocent blood, a heart that devises wicked plans, feet that are swift in running to evil, a false witness who speaks lies, and one who sows discord among brethren." (Proverbs 6:16-19)*

160

Notice the poetic structure: six things the Lord hates, but the seventh is an abomination above all—one who sows discord among brethren. Psalm 133 celebrates how good and pleasant it is for brethren to dwell together in unity. The opposite is someone who destroys that unity.

How to Deal with Conflict

When an issue arises—someone says something hurtful, someone does something wrong, or gossip and slander are encountered—Matthew 18 provides the pattern:

> *"Moreover if your brother sins against you, go and tell him his fault between you and him alone. If he hears you, you have gained your brother. But if he will not hear, take with you one or two more, that 'by the mouth of two or three witnesses every word may be established.'" (Matthew 18:15-16)*

Before following these steps, however, there is an important first response: take it to the Lord. Pray about it and see if God gives peace and understanding. Perhaps God will open new eyes to see with love, to hope all things, and to believe the best about that person. Perhaps the conclusion will be, "They did not mean it the way it sounded," and peace will settle the matter.

But if peace does not come, then go to that person privately. Not to friends. Not to The Church. Not to neighbors. Privately. If they listen, the brother or sister is gained. If not, then bring one or two more—preferably elders or mature believers from The Church, people who can help establish what occurred.

The principle applies broadly: if there is an issue bothering anyone with any person or situation, take it to the Lord first. If peace comes, the matter is resolved. If peace does not come, unresolved conflict sets the stage for bitterness—and Hebrews 12 warns that a root of bitterness defiles many. Imagine if believers dealt with issues as they arose, coming together with no baggage, no awkwardness, no unresolved tension—simply dealing with matters and, when necessary, bringing others alongside to help rather than allowing resentment to build and create disunity.

The Rest of the List

> *"...without self-control, brutal, despisers of good, traitors, headstrong, haughty, lovers of pleasure rather than lovers of God."*
> *(2 Timothy 3:3-4)*

On that last point—lovers of pleasure rather than lovers of God—Satan appears to be attacking The Church on two fronts. First, he works to isolate Christians. In this age, a person could never leave the house. Everything needed can be delivered. Church can be watched online. People can hole up at home indefinitely—something impossible even for the youngest adults in their own childhood. In just the last several years, staying home with everything delivered and endless entertainment available has become normal.

Second, people love their amusement. There are times when any honest believer must admit: "I could be reading a book that builds my faith, or I could watch this television show"—and sometimes the television show wins. That is not inherently wrong, but consider this: 150 years ago, what amusement options existed? Many people did not even have a radio. No television, no internet, nothing. So people read their Bibles. The temptation was not there.

Believers today live in an age of unprecedented distraction. Know this: very perilous, difficult, hard-to-bear times will come in the last days. Yet everyone alive today was born for such a time as this. As Paul proclaimed on Mars Hill in Acts 17, everyone is born where and when they were born so that they might reach out after God. God placed each person in a time and place where He believed success was possible. If God believed believers could succeed in such a brutal time, then they must be equipped to do so.

The first half of chapter 3 addresses perilous times and perilous people. The second half reveals the remedy: the man of God and the Word of God.

A Form of Godliness

> *"having a form of godliness but denying its*
> *power. And from such people turn away!"*
> *(2 Timothy 3:5)*

It is one thing to surround oneself with Christians. It is another thing entirely to surround oneself with holy, godly people. Christians are not hard to find. But truly godly people—those who challenge and uplift, who will stop mid-sentence to pray—are not as easy to find. Yet surrounding oneself with such people makes a transformative difference. Their influence rubs off. Conversely, surrounding oneself with ungodly people—or even ungodly entertainment—has effects as well. Constant immersion in certain vocabulary, themes, and ideas inevitably leaves a mark. Turn away from those who merely talk the talk but do not help in the walk, and cling to Spirit-filled believers who build others up.

Gullible Women and False Teachers

> *"For of this sort are those who creep into*
> *households and make captives of gullible*

women loaded down with sins, led away by
various lusts, always learning and never
able to come to the knowledge of the truth."
(2 Timothy 3:6-7)

Paul specifically warns about false teachers who target women. The word "gullible" is in the text—Paul wrote it. As 1 Timothy 2:14 states, "Adam was not deceived, but the woman being deceived, fell into transgression." This is not what the world wants to hear, but men and women are different.

Women often have a stronger draw toward spiritual things—a more natural desire to learn and grow in the things of the Lord. Men tend to be more reluctant; they often need more encouragement. But because of that natural spiritual draw, women can be more susceptible to false teaching. This is why Satan targeted Eve. Men often go off and sin knowing exactly what they are doing; women are more often deceived. This is not true of every woman, but it is a biblical pattern.

Consider a woman interested in the things of the Lord whose husband does not teach her because he is not spiritually engaged. She seeks teaching elsewhere—and today, going online provides both excellent teaching and garbage. Without brothers and sisters who can speak into her life, she can be carried away. The word "lusts" here does not necessarily mean sexual desire; it simply means desires—the desire to learn and grow. Someone comes along teaching, she embraces his teaching, and deception follows.

"Always learning and never able to come to the knowledge of the truth" describes people—men and women alike—who constantly seek something new. They want anyone who will teach them something different. Yet sound teaching has not changed. What is taught today from Scripture could be found 100 years ago. Nothing is new. But certain people are attracted to novelty:

> *"For all the Athenians and the foreigners*
> *who were there spent their time in nothing*
> *else but either to tell or to hear some new*
> *thing." (Acts 17:21)*

This leads people into false teaching because "I have never heard it taught this way before" sounds intriguing. "This is secret teaching that other pastors have not figured out" appeals to the desire for novelty. But truth is not novel.

Jannes and Jambres

> *"Now as Jannes and Jambres resisted*
> *Moses, so do these also resist the truth: men*
> *of corrupt minds, disapproved concerning*
> *the faith; but they will progress no further,*
> *for their folly will be manifest to all, as*
> *theirs also was." (2 Timothy 3:8-9)*

The Targum of Jonathan, Josephus, and other ancient writings identify Jannes and Jambres as the sorcerers of Pharaoh in Exodus 7-8. Their names do not appear in the Old Testament, but Jewish tradition and early Christian sources consistently identify them this way. In Exodus, Aaron threw down his rod and it became a serpent; the sorcerers threw down their rods and their rods also became serpents—but Aaron's rod swallowed theirs. The sorcerers turned water into blood; they brought forth frogs. But when it came to the plague of lice in Exodus 8:18-19, they said, "This is the finger of God." They had reached the limit of their power.

Paul's point is that false teachers, like those sorcerers, will eventually be exposed. Their folly will become manifest to all, just as it did in Egypt when the one true God demonstrated His supremacy.

The Man of God and the Word of God

> *"But you have carefully followed my doctrine, manner of life, purpose, faith, longsuffering, love, perseverance, persecutions, afflictions, which happened to me at Antioch, at Iconium, at Lystra—what persecutions I endured. And out of them all the Lord delivered me!" (2 Timothy 3:10-11)*

"Carefully followed" translates *parakolouthéō* (παρακολουθέω). The root *akolouthos* means "follower"—the origin of the English word "acolyte." Paul adds *para* (alongside) for emphasis: Timothy was an alongside-follower who watched all of Paul's ways.

One time while teaching at my old church, I saw an elderly couple—the husband was a mentor of mine in my early years in the faith. I could look through the room and identify people who had impressed upon me so much: here were people from nearly twenty years earlier who had shaped my walk. I remember being in this older couple's home when some nasty news story came up. People began discussing it, and the wife asked for details. The husband simply said, "We do not even need to talk about that. We all know there is wickedness and evil in this world. We do not need the details. We do not need to dwell on that. We need to focus." That stuck with me. As Psalm 101 says, "I will not know evil." This man's example of leading his home impressed me deeply.

More is caught than taught. Believers learn much from
Scripture, but surrounding oneself with godly, Spirit-filled,
mature, zealous Christians has a profound effect. Their
influence wears off on others. Timothy carefully followed
Paul's doctrine, manner of life, purpose, faith,
longsuffering, love, perseverance, persecutions, and
afflictions. May every believer be able to say to younger
Christians, "Imitate me as I imitate Christ. You are
watching me." Timothy watched Paul and learned from
him.

Antioch, Iconium, and Lystra were Timothy's home
region—the very places where Paul was stoned and left for
dead, then got up and went back into the city. Timothy
remembered all that Paul endured there.

Persecution for Godliness

> *"Yes, and all who desire to live godly in
> Christ Jesus will suffer persecution."*
> *(2 Timothy 3:12)*

> *"Remember the word that I said to you, 'A
> servant is not greater than his master.' If
> they persecuted Me, they will also persecute
> you." (John 15:20)*

Those who desire to live godly in Christ Jesus will suffer
persecution. There are implications here: if someone does
not want to suffer persecution, there is a solution—and it is
not to abandon Christianity, but simply to avoid being
godly about it. A person can be saved, barely scraping into
heaven, and avoid persecution. But those who want to be
godly will draw attention, rub people wrong, and upset
others when taking a stand for what is righteous, good, and
holy.

167

*"But evil men and impostors will grow
worse and worse, deceiving and being
deceived." (2 Timothy 3:13)*

Things are not going to get better in these perilous last
days. As 2 Peter 3:3 warns, "Scoffers will come in the last
days, walking according to their own lusts." They are
willfully ignorant—as one teacher I used to follow put it,
"dumb on purpose"—because they want to serve their own
desires. They do not want God telling them what to do. It
will get worse. Believers should not expect things overall to
improve.

Continue in What You Have Learned

*"But you must continue in the things which
you have learned and been assured of,
knowing from whom you have learned them,
and that from childhood you have known the
Holy Scriptures, which are able to make you
wise for salvation through faith which is in
Christ Jesus." (2 Timothy 3:14-15)*

Timothy had Lois and Eunice—his grandmother and
mother—and he had Paul himself. Timothy had excellent
teachers, and it is a blessing to see people who taught in the
faith still going strong, still on the same course, providing
footsteps to follow.

Interestingly, "Scriptures" here is *grammata* (γράμματα)—
meaning letters or written characters—rather than the usual
graphē (writings). This is the only place this word is
translated "Scriptures" in the New Testament. One scholar,
R.C.H. Lenski, suggests Paul may be indicating that
Timothy learned to read from the Scriptures themselves—
that he learned even the letters of the alphabet through the

sacred text. Generations past often learned to read from the Bible because it was the one book in the house.

Chuck Smith used to say his mother read the Bible to him when he was still in the cradle. Children cannot understand it—whether King James or any other translation—but pouring Scripture into them matters. My own children listen to Bible chapters every day. Right now we are going through Job, and they have no idea what is happening. But they hear it, and they will hear it again and again. Sometimes we pause to summarize: "Remember, Job is hurting right now, so he is going to say some strange things. And his friends have good intentions but are a bit confused." Then we continue. The point is simply pouring Scripture into children.

All Scripture Is God-Breathed

> *"All Scripture is given by inspiration of God, and is profitable for doctrine, for reproof, for correction, for instruction in righteousness, that the man of God may be complete, thoroughly equipped for every good work." (2 Timothy 3:16-17)*

"Given by inspiration of God" is *theopneustos* (θεόπνευστος)—literally "God-breathed," combining *theos* (God) and *pneō* (to breathe, related to *pneuma*, spirit). "God-breathed" is a very literal translation. All Scripture— every single word, every jot and tittle—is God-breathed.

Scripture is profitable for *reproof*. This is *elegchos* (ἔλεγχος)—a proof, conviction, or evidence. The technical sense of "proof" as used in mathematics is illuminating: a logical sequence of steps demonstrating truth by relying on known facts, axioms, and established rules, effectively showing that a statement is undeniably true based on solid reasoning. The Bible functions the same way. Scripture can be used to logically unfold truth, step by step, showing beyond reasonable doubt what is true. It uncovers and convicts because it demonstrates what is undeniably so.

Scripture is profitable for *correction*. This is *epanorthōsis* (ἐπανόρθωσις)—to restore to an upright position. Something has fallen; this sets it back up where it belongs.

Scripture is profitable for *instruction*. This is *paideia* (παιδεία), which appears six times in the New Testament— four times translated "chastisement" (discipline, training). The word encompasses the whole training and education of children. A local Christian school in our community is named Paideia for this reason. Scripture provides complete instruction in righteousness.

Consider the flow: someone needs to be shown that the Bible is true, that God's way is true. Reproof demonstrates the problem. Then correction sets the person back upright. Then instruction thrusts them forward. Through this process, the man of God is made complete.

"Complete" is *artios* (ἄρτιος)—a rare word meaning complete or perfect, with "reference apparently to special aptitude for given use." It derives from an adverb meaning "just now, at this very moment." The sense is being ready to be used—complete and ready. Every person was fearfully and wonderfully made for a purpose, and when God does this work, He brings people back to where they are able and ready to be used again. Perhaps someone has thrown things away or gotten off track, but the Word of God can restore usefulness—that special aptitude for the purpose God designed.

"Thoroughly equipped" is *exartizō* (ἐξαρτίζω)—*ek* (out of) plus *artios*. Paul emphasizes the point: the Word of God makes believers fit for the Master's use, ready to be used by God, thoroughly ready for every good work He wants to accomplish through them.

> *"...as His divine power has given to us all things that pertain to life and godliness, through the knowledge of Him who called us by glory and virtue." (2 Peter 1:3)*

The Charge to Timothy

> *"I charge you therefore before God and the Lord Jesus Christ, who will judge the living and the dead at His appearing and His kingdom: Preach the word! Be ready in season and out of season. Convince, rebuke, exhort, with all longsuffering and teaching."*
> *(2 Timothy 4:1-2)*

"I charge you." This is Paul speaking to Timothy. If Timothy were present, he would sit at attention. "I charge you therefore before God and the Lord Jesus Christ, who will judge the living and the dead at His appearing and His kingdom." The weight of this charge cannot be overstated.

"Preach" is *kēryssō* (κηρύσσω)—the primary word for preaching in the New Testament. Of its sixty-one occurrences, it consistently refers to proclamation directed at unbelievers. Teaching occurred among believers, among the disciples, but when going out to reach the lost, it was always this heralding—calling people to the kingdom of God. "Preach the word"—because one cannot simply preach thoughts and feelings. The Word of God must be proclaimed.

"Convince, rebuke, exhort." These three align with what Scripture accomplishes. *Convince* (*elegchō*) means to

171

convict, expose, bring to light, show fault. First, show people that they are sinners. Jonathan Edwards preached "Sinners in the Hands of an Angry God." *Rebuke* (*epitimaō*) literally means to tax or issue a penalty—to charge someone with wrongdoing and show them the consequence. Step one: "You are sinners." Step two: "The wages of sin is death." *Exhort* (*parakaleō*) means to call to one's side, to comfort, console, and strengthen. If people can be shown they are sinners and that the wages of sin is death—and they believe those two truths—they will be ready to hear the comforting call, the exhortation, the gospel.

Itching Ears

> *"For the time will come when they will not endure sound doctrine, but according to their own desires, because they have itching ears, they will heap up for themselves teachers; and they will turn their ears away from the truth, and be turned aside to fables." (2 Timothy 4:3-4)*

It is almost too disheartening to joke about. Are there not countless churches and pastors—on television, in towns everywhere—who exist simply to tell people what they want to hear? People want churches where they hear something that makes them feel good, that lets them check The Church box and continue happily with their lives. They do not want sound doctrine. Heaven forbid they hear something that rubs them wrong—that would mean they are not perfect. But every time the Word of God is opened, some of it should rub believers wrong, unless they have already attained perfection.

"Fables" is *mythos* (μῦθος)—myths, narratives, stories. There will be pastors in the last days who prefer telling stories to preaching the Word. If one had a nickel for every pastor who did more storytelling than Word-preaching, one could probably buy a burger—and that represents a lot of nickels these days. This is what the last days look like: people want stories; they do not want the Word.

> *"But you be watchful in all things, endure*
> *afflictions, do the work of an evangelist,*
> *fulfill your ministry." (2 Timothy 4:5)*

"Do the work of an evangelist, fulfill your ministry." Timothy was not called to be an evangelist, but he was called to do the work of one. Sometimes everyone must step up and fill gaps. Someone might say, "I am not called to that ministry," but the work still needs doing—so step up. At the same time, do not forget to fulfill your own ministry. Find what God has called you to and pour into that as well. Be a gap-filler who is willing to step in wherever there is need, while also discovering and pursuing God's specific calling.

Paul's Farewell

> *"For I am already being poured out as a*
> *drink offering, and the time of my departure*
> *is at hand. I have fought the good fight, I*
> *have finished the race, I have kept the faith."*
> *(2 Timothy 4:6-7)*

Paul knows his death is near. He obviously expects to live long enough for Timothy to bring the items he requests—otherwise he would not ask—but he knows the end is approaching. A drink offering (libation) was poured out as described in Exodus, Leviticus, and Numbers. Paul sees himself being poured out, with only an empty vessel remaining when the pouring is complete.

"I have fought the good fight, I have finished the race, I have kept the faith." Will every believer be able to say that? Many will not finish the race. Many will not keep the faith to the very end. And can one truly say "I have kept the faith" without having fought the fight? Someone may have believed unto salvation, but the full gravity of salvation—the reality of the lost, the promise of heavenly reward—should drive believers to fight the fight all the way to the end. There is something deeply admirable about that. "Well done, good and faithful servant. You have been faithful over a few things, I will make you ruler over many things. Enter into the joy of your lord" (Matthew 25:21).

The Crown of Righteousness

> *"Finally, there is laid up for me the crown of righteousness, which the Lord, the righteous Judge, will give to me on that Day, and not to me only but also to all who have loved His appearing." (2 Timothy 4:8)*

"Crown" is *stephanos* (στέφανος)—not the royal diadem (*diadēma*) but the laurel wreath, the victor's crown given to winners in the Olympic games. In Revelation 19:12, Jesus wears many *diadems*—kingly crowns. But this is the victor's crown, the reward for those who finish the race.

Scripture mentions five heavenly crowns:

First, the Imperishable Crown (1 Corinthians 9:25): "Everyone who competes for the prize is temperate in all things. Now they do it to obtain a perishable crown, but we for an imperishable crown."

Second, the Crown of Rejoicing (1 Thessalonians 2:19): "For what is our hope, or joy, or crown of rejoicing? Is it not even you in the presence of our Lord Jesus Christ at His coming?" Many believe this refers to the moment when God wipes away every tear—the crown of finally rejoicing in the presence of the Lord Jesus.

Third, the Crown of Righteousness (2 Timothy 4:8): The reward for fighting hard and fighting to the end.

Fourth, the Crown of Glory (1 Peter 5:4): "When the Chief Shepherd appears, you will receive the crown of glory that does not fade away." In context, this appears to be specifically for elders—those who not only served but rose to lead The Church. "If a man desires the position of a bishop, he desires a good work" (1 Timothy 3:1), but "let not many of you become teachers, knowing that we shall receive a stricter judgment" (James 3:1). It is not easy, and poor teaching brings judgment—but for those who do it well, there is a crown.

Fifth, the Crown of Life (Revelation 2:10): "Do not fear any of those things which you are about to suffer. Indeed, the devil is about to throw some of you into prison, that you may be tested, and you will have tribulation ten days. Be faithful until death, and I will give you the crown of life." Many believe this is the crown of the martyr—a special reward for faithfulness unto death.

These five crowns should not be approached legalistically or dogmatically—they are simply five crowns mentioned in Scripture that can be titled based on their contexts. But one day there will be a heavenly gathering, and the more crowns one has, the more opportunities to cast them at Christ's feet. That is worth striving for.

Russ Phillips, the world champion horseshoe player from our town who is now with the Lord, once inspired a thought about that day: perhaps there will be a heavenly game of horseshoes—the more crowns, the more throws at the

Master's feet. He is getting extra practice now, which seems unfair.

Demas and Mark: A Study in Contrasts

> *"Be diligent to come to me quickly; for*
> *Demas has forsaken me, having loved this*
> *present world, and has departed for*
> *Thessalonica." (2 Timothy 4:9-10)*

Demas appears in Colossians 4:14 and Philemon, listed among faithful workers with great accolades. In Philemon, he is mentioned next to Aristarchus, who was from Thessalonica—suggesting Demas may have been from there as well. Perhaps he simply went home. The text does not say Demas left the faith, but he left Paul. He had been serving in one of the most respectable and honorable positions of ministry—alongside Paul the Apostle—but because of the love of the world, he let it go. He gave up what could have been great reward and great honor because the world got hold of him.

Know this: in the last days, perilous, almost unbearable times will come. For Demas, it was the love of the world. For those who love themselves, the world becomes very attractive.

> *"...that their hearts may be knit together in*
> *love." (Colossians 2:2)*

When people serve together, a bond forms—similar to the bond on a battlefield, the bond of fighting together and going through the trenches together. People become very close, which makes it all the more painful when someone departs. Over the years, I have seen those who stood at my right and at my left in ministry—and then time passes, and they are no longer there. It is heartbreaking because of the bond formed in that relationship.

"Demas has forsaken me, having loved this present world." They used to serve together, travel together, do ministry together, pray together, stay up late together, discuss Scripture together. But now he has other priorities. He has gone to do his own thing. Yet Paul has fought the good fight, finished the race, and kept the faith. No matter how many people abandon him, Paul will stay the course.

Crescens went to Galatia (he is mentioned only here in Scripture). Titus went to Dalmatia (perhaps he was pastor to the 101 Dalmatians).

> *"Only Luke is with me. Get Mark and bring him with you, for he is useful to me for ministry." (2 Timothy 4:11)*

Mark—John Mark—is the one who abandoned Paul and Barnabas on the first missionary journey. In Acts 15, when they were about to set out on the second journey, Barnabas (Mark's relative) wanted to bring him along, but Paul refused. "He bailed on us. I do not want a deserter on the team." The contention grew so sharp—the same Greek word (*paroxysmos*) used in Hebrews 10:24 for "stirring up" love and good works describes their irritation—that they parted ways. Barnabas took Mark to Cyprus, and tradition holds they did ministry there before eventually moving elsewhere.

Years later, Paul writes: "Get Mark and bring him with you, for he is useful to me for ministry." Mark failed miserably early in his ministry. His idol—Paul the Apostle, the rising star—had torn him down, essentially saying, "I do not want you if you come along." That had to hurt.

177

Early in my faith, I was leading worship at a home study. I had played guitar for many years and enjoyed singing, but I had never led worship in a church setting. A pastor whom I highly admired told me that he would rather have no singing at all than have me lead worship. It was a heavy hit—probably very similar to what Mark felt when Paul the Apostle did not want him around. I wanted to quit and never lead worship again. I am glad I did not quit. I am glad I kept going. I had to learn a lot about leading worship, because a person can be good at music and not good at leading worship—they are very different things. I have seen many great musicians who are horrible worship leaders because they do not understand that they are not just singing and performing; they are leading people in corporate worship. I had played music, but I had never led worship. There was much to learn.

Here is the moral: Mark began as a deserter, but he stuck with it and ended up being someone useful. Demas started off as someone very useful with great accolades, but he ended up being a deserter. If anyone has a history of being a Demas, take heart—it is possible to end up like Mark. But if anyone is a "Mark" right now, be warned: it is possible to turn out like Demas. It can go either way. Past failures and mistakes do not disqualify anyone permanently. Stick with it, and usefulness to God will follow—equipped for every good work. But no one has arrived at the point where they can coast to the finish line. Paul had to fight the good fight of faith and press on in his race.

Tychicus: The Willing and Able Servant

"And Tychicus I have sent to Ephesus."
(2 Timothy 4:12)

Tychicus is not a household name, but examining the verses about him reveals much. He delivered the letters to the Ephesians, Colossians, and Philemon. He was one of two candidates to replace Titus in Crete (as mentioned in the book of Titus). Here, Paul sends him to Ephesus to enable Timothy to come.

Paul wanted Timothy, but Timothy had important work. Someone equipped to fill the gap was needed—and that someone was Tychicus. What emerges from these small verses is a portrait of a man who was always willing to go. He left Paul to deliver letters; he was the top candidate to go to Crete; he went to Ephesus. He was a willing servant. He was also a qualified servant—Paul was not entrusting the letter to the Ephesians to just anyone, and he would not choose just anyone to replace Titus or Timothy.

Here is someone without the fame and accolades of better-known biblical figures—but a servant who was willing and able. That is a worthy aspiration: to be willing to go whenever asked, and to be equipped, prepared, and worthy to take on the task.

The Cloak and the Parchments

"Bring the cloak that I left with Carpus at Troas when you come—and the books, especially the parchments."
(2 Timothy 4:13)

The cloak was a heavy garment—more like a cape or poncho, a large blanket with a hole for the head. It was for winter. Paul likely left it behind while traveling in summer because of its weight, but now he was in prison and winter was approaching. In verse 21 he writes, "Do your utmost to come before winter." He wanted his coat back.

The word "books" is *biblion* (βιβλίον)—the diminutive of *biblos*, a papyrus scroll. The diminutive form (like adding

179

"-ito" in Spanish to make something small—*burro* becomes *burrito*) indicates smaller pieces of scrolls. Papyrus was made from a plant, and these were likely smaller documents—perhaps a journal, perhaps letters Paul had received from the churches (the Corinthian correspondence reveals ongoing exchange of letters), perhaps copies of portions of the New Testament. Whatever they were, they were precious to him.

But more importantly, Paul asks for "the parchments"—*membrana* (μεμβράνα)—paper made from dried animal skin. A good friend of mine in Israel, who is a Jewish sofer (scribe), has done demonstrations for our groups when we visit. He explained the process: everything must be natural—the ink, the pens made from animal quills, and the paper itself from animal skin. This is what the Old Testament Scriptures were written on.

When Paul says, "Bring the cloak... and the books, but *especially* the parchments," he is saying: "I may die any day now. The cloak would be nice—it is going to get cold. I do want those books. But what I really want is my Scriptures."

It is doubtful Paul possessed an entire Old Testament—the cost would have been enormous, and the scrolls nearly impossible to carry (the Torah alone is massive). But he probably had portions of Old Testament Scripture that he treasured. In the last moments of his life, he wanted his Scripture nearby.

Alexander the Coppersmith

"Alexander the coppersmith did me much harm. May the Lord repay him according to his works. You also must beware of him, for

he has greatly resisted our words."
(2 Timothy 4:14-15)

This Alexander is likely not the same as others mentioned in Scripture—it was an extremely common name because of Alexander the Great. Paul names him directly. He was not afraid to identify a clear bad guy. When warning The Church about genuinely harmful people, naming names is appropriate. Alexander had greatly resisted the gospel message, and The Church needed to beware of him.

Paul's First Defense

"At my first defense no one stood with me,
but all forsook me. May it not be charged
against them." (2 Timothy 4:16)

"Defense" is a legal term for a trial. Paul went to trial because he was in prison, and no one was willing to stand up for him. It appears Alexander was the one bringing charges, and when no one contested them—when you could hear a pin drop—people were afraid. To stand up and defend Paul would be to join him in his fate. So Paul graciously says, "May it not be charged against them. They were afraid, and that is understandable. But this man making false claims? Be on guard against him."

"But the Lord stood with me and
strengthened me, so that the message might
be preached fully through me, and that all
the Gentiles might hear. And I was delivered
out of the mouth of the lion. And the Lord
will deliver me from every evil work and
preserve me for His heavenly kingdom. To
Him be glory forever and ever. Amen!"
(2 Timothy 4:17-18)

181

"Delivered out of the mouth of the lion"—commentators have debated this phrase. Paul would not have been thrown to lions; as a Roman citizen, he would have been beheaded. Many Christians were thrown to lions in the Colosseum, but not Roman citizens. The phrase is figurative, picturing imminent danger. Jesus delivered Paul so that he was not immediately executed. He had time to write this letter and continue ministry a while longer. God delivered him, and God would deliver him all the way into His kingdom. Paul knew God would keep him until the end.

Final Greetings

> "Greet Prisca and Aquila, and the household of Onesiphorus. Erastus stayed in Corinth, but Trophimus I have left in Miletus sick." (2 Timothy 4:19-20)

"Prisca" is Priscilla—Prisca being the formal name, Priscilla the more casual form (like Joseph and Joe). These final greetings provide geographical details that help reconstruct Paul's final journey, as discussed in the introduction to this letter.

"Trophimus I have left in Miletus sick." This small detail carries doctrinal significance. Some teach that Christians should never be sick, or that faith can always produce healing—that if healing does not occur, faith is insufficient. But Paul the Apostle had to leave Trophimus in Miletus because he was sick. Paul could not heal him.

Consider the evidence: when Epaphroditus came to Paul in prison (recorded in Philippians), he nearly died and Paul thought he would lose him. Timothy had stomach problems, and Paul's prescription was wine with his water—why not simply mail him a healing handkerchief, like those in Acts that healed people? The Bible paints a clear picture: even the godliest and most powerfully used people did not always have access to miraculous power on demand. God moved, and they did miracles; God did not move, and miracles did not happen. If Paul could have healed Trophimus, he surely would have. They almost certainly prayed for healing, but it did not happen. This is a small doctrinal nugget, but it is there, and it is good to have these verses when someone teaches otherwise.

> *"Do your utmost to come before winter.*
> *Eubulus greets you, as well as Pudens,*
> *Linus, Claudia, and all the brethren."*
> *(2 Timothy 4:21)*

These are names about which little is known—except for Linus. Paul writes from Rome, from a Roman prison. Early church fathers taught that this Linus became the bishop of Rome after Peter, and the Catholic Church numbers him among the early popes. This is a fairly common early church belief. Early church fathers made mistakes, of course, so it should be taken with a grain of salt. But it is fascinating when names appear in Scripture that the early church knew more about and could provide details the Bible does not.

> *"The Lord Jesus Christ be with your spirit.*
> *Grace be with you. Amen." (2 Timothy 4:22)*

Conclusion

It is bittersweet to come to the end of Paul's letters. This is such a powerful section of text, filled with warnings for the last days. But let it be said again, lest anyone forget:

Know this. Do not be ignorant. In the last days, difficult, unbearable, almost impossible times will come. But believers have come for such a time as this.

The Pastoral Epistles

Continue in the things you have learned. That word "continue" is *menō*—to abide, to remain. Abide in the vine. Remain immovable. Every believer knows what they ought to be doing. Stick with it. Hold fast. So that when the race is finished, you, I, and every believer can say:

"I have fought the good fight, I have finished the race, I have kept the faith."

About Revival Church

Revival Church is a Bible-believing fellowship in Grandview, Washington, committed to the faithful teaching of God's Word, the simplicity of New Testament worship, and the call to live out the Gospel in everyday life.

Our desire is to see believers grow in their knowledge of Scripture, be equipped for the work of ministry, and walk in faithfulness until Christ returns. We believe the local church is the pillar and ground of the truth, and that sound doctrine must always produce godly living. In 2025 we completed our journey of teaching verse by verse through the Bible and began to do it again.

If you are ever in the Lower Yakima Valley and looking for a church home, or simply passing through, we would be honored to have you join us.

You can see our most up to date service times on our website:

TheRevival.Church

"I have no greater joy than to hear that my children walk in truth." —3 John 4

www.ingramcontent.com/pod-product-compliance
Lightning Source LLC
Chambersburg PA
CBHW061747120626
46550CB00005B/1914